Anne Therese Naylor has a Bachelor of Education, a Master of Special Education and accreditation as a NAATI Paraprofessional Auslan Interpreter. She is passionate about literacy and throughout her career has had the privilege and joy of teaching deaf children to read and write through sign language.

Anne began writing after her third child was born in 1987. Her poignant story 'I had a Down syndrome baby at 27' was awarded second prize in a non-fiction writing competition and published in Cosmopolitan in July, 2000.

In 2005, an intense desire to paint was accompanied by the onset of bipolar disorder. Anne's allegorical work 'What lies beneath' was awarded first prize in the 2008 Central Coast Mental Health Artworks Exhibition.

A mental health and disability advocate, Anne is a Carer Representative for Carers NSW. She is dedicated to raising awareness, challenging stereotypes and fighting the stigma of disability and mental illness.

Glass House Books
Brisbane

Art from Adversity:
A Life with Bipolar

Anne Therese Naylor

Glass House Books
Brisbane

Glass House Books
an imprint of IP (Interactive Publications Pty Ltd)
Treetop Studio • 9 Kuhler Court
Carindale, Queensland, Australia 4152
sales@ipoz.biz
ipoz.biz/GHB/GHB.htm

First published by IP in 2013
© Anne Therese Naylor, 2013

Printed in 11 pt Book Antiqua on 14 pt Book Antiqua.

National Library of Australia
Cataloguing-in-Publication entry:

Author: Naylor, Anne Therese.

Title: Art from adversity : a life with bipolar / Anne Therese Naylor.

ISBN: 9781922120113 (pbk.)

Subjects: Naylor, Anne Therese.
           Manic-depressive persons--Biography.
           Manic-depressive illness.

Dewey Number: 616.895092

*This book is dedicated to those who have a mental illness,
and to those who support them.*

Acknowledgments

Cover Images: 'Firestorm' by Anne Naylor (front cover); 'You're not alone' by Anne Naylor (back cover); 'Inland rivers' by Anne Naylor (back cover)

Jacket Design: David P Reiter

Author Photos: Wayne Cheung

With love and gratitude, I'd like to acknowledge the following people for their personal support and for their contributions to this book:

David, Lauren and Anna from Interactive Publications, Irena from ID Editing and Publishing, Damien from Newbie Writers, authors Mike and Topo, and Monica, who helped me realise my dream of having this book published.

Deidre, Greg, Brian, Vija and Mary Ann, who helped save my sanity.

Ernie, who taught me how to paint and who photographed some of the artworks in this book. Wayne Cheung for his photographic contributions.

The Solar Springs Down syndrome mothers, who encouraged and inspired me.

Kay Redfield Jamison and the many writers and researchers, who continue to shed their own special light on bipolar disorder.

My Wilson Island friends, Mary-Anne, John, Genevieve (may she rest in peace), Paul, Sandra, Wayne, Peter, Julie, Mark and Yvonne, who shared the best three days of my life.

My friends Trish, Rolla, Jill, Gabrielle, Laisarn, Bev, Charles, Greg, Dany, Bernadette, Stephen, Lisa and Mona, who remind me how lucky I am.

My mother-in-law and my extended family, who love and support me.

Joan (in memorium), Moira, Rebecca and the Tuesday girls, who were there when I needed them.

My mother, and my father, who are each an inspiration, and my siblings, who I love dearly.

M, T, S, H, and everyone else who battles bipolar.

My children, Michelle, Alison, Josh and Tom who I cherish, and who make me proud.

And most of all Mal, who I love more than anyone.

Contents

Introduction

This book

This book is for anyone interested in mental health and/or people who like to read memoirs. It is a human story with universal themes, as much as it is a story about mental illness.

Part I: Memoir is a collection of vignettes. Stories. My stories. Well some of them anyway. They will give you an insight into what it's like to have a mental illness and they will take you to unfamiliar places, or perhaps to places you know only too well.

The stories in this book are all true, and the people and places are real. However, I have changed names (and on occasion gender and occupation) out of respect for those who are sensitive to the stigma surrounding mental illness and do who not wish to be identified.

Part II: Bipolar disorder consists of information about bipolar disorder but also mental illness in general. This is not an academic text and it is not substitute for medical advice. However, it is (hopefully) educational, informative and enlightening in its own way.

I am not a scientist or doctor so if you have any concerns about your own mental health, or that of someone you know, please see a professional. I do, however, live with bipolar disorder, so I feel very qualified to write about it.

In the eyes of society to have bipolar disorder is a tragedy, a devastating occurrence that will inevitably lead to a life of suffering for all concerned. And that *is* true for some, but not for everyone. Not for me.

Having bipolar disorder is not all doom and misery. There are many positive aspects if you are willing to look for them. There are also a lot of fun (and funny) things about it.

Not only should we be able to talk about mental illness, we should be able to cry and laugh and rejoice in it too.

Artworks: All of the artworks in this book are my own. I was not a visual artist before becoming ill with bipolar and I had no previous training, skills or experience in fine arts.

When I was (unknowingly) becoming manic, I decided I wanted to paint.

The intense drive to paint and draw arrived with hypomania, stayed through melancholy, and departed with the medication and management of my bipolar disorder. It came as suddenly and mysteriously as it went.

I adorned the walls of my house with my paintings where they remain today, a testament to the fleeting beauty of bipolar.

Fireworks - Oil on canvas 450 x 600 mm

Part 1:

Memoir

'The statistics on sanity are that one out of every four people are suffering from some form of mental illness. Think of your three best friends. If they're OK, then it's you.'

Rita Mae Brown

Prologue

A sojourn in the South Pacific

The South Pacific was calling.

Did I really want to go?

I didn't need to think about it, my answer was yes. Yes. A week away by myself was just what I needed. I had talked myself into it and now I had to convince everyone else.

I begged and pleaded. My husband said if it was that important to me, I should go. He was concerned about the cost, but said we would find the money somehow. He was supportive, as always, and I loved him for it. He assured me he'd be fine looking after the house and the children. After all, I'd only be gone for seven days.

I had great expectations and high hopes for this trip, but I was nervous too. I had never been away from my family for a whole week before.

Upon arrival I checked in at reception. I had been assigned a room at the rear, which was disappointing. I would have much preferred one of the front suites, with views out over the ocean. The elegant woman behind the desk was most apologetic. She said she'd see what she could do.

I unpacked my bags and went for a walk. The place was surrounded by an exquisitely beautiful natural environment. It was the perfect time of year. The skies were blue, the temperatures warm and the breezes cool. The beach was stunning. During the day birds screeched and squawked and at night I could hear the waves gently lapping the shore.

I introduced myself to the other guests who shared my table at meal times. We talked about many things, including why we had been drawn to the South Pacific and what we hoped to discover about ourselves while we were there.

Behind his dark glasses, I recognised a well-known footballer. He was staying at the same place too. I wanted to ask for his autograph, but I didn't. I thought it might be intrusive.

Despite having people around, I was lonely and missed my family. Nevertheless, I knew I should make the most of the break. I would be home soon enough.

My memories of the South Pacific are now faded and fragmented, however I still remember some things clearly. Good things, like the huge, deep bath in the spa room, the comfortable guest lounge, the special blends of herbal tea and the leisurely walks along the beach.

I have unhappy memories too, like my overwhelming sense of isolation and all-consuming feelings of disconnection, dislocation and disorientation.

That was my sojourn in the South Pacific. South Pacific Private Hospital, that is. It was the psychiatric facility I had chosen for my week away.

South Pacific Private (SPP) is not the type of place I would normally have chosen to visit, and my time there was far from idyllic. It was, quite possibly, the worst week of my life, but it was also the beginning of my recovery.

No offence to SPP, it is a wonderful place, but when the time comes for my next sojourn, I hope it will be the other South Pacific calling.

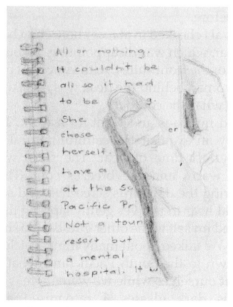

The South Pacific - Pencil on paper 140 x 210 mm

4

Beginning

My autobiography

My childhood was happy and carefree

The world was a simple, safe place
and my parents loved me

School was pretty good
and I had a few friends

I felt weird at times in primary school
but doesn't everyone?

I had a few problems in high school
but don't most people?

I met the love of my life when I was seventeen
went to uni, became a teacher, got married and had four
children

In my mid-thirties I went back to uni
got a Master's degree and went back to work

Ten years later
I was diagnosed with bipolar disorder

I am now a member of an exclusive club
and in very good company

Agatha Christie, Sylvia Plath and Virginia Woolf
Nina Simone, Sting and Brian Wilson

Vivienne Leigh, Carrie Fisher and Catherine Zeta-Jones
… just to name a few

These days I do the same things everyone else does
I spend time with my family and friends and I go to work

I'm lucky
Life is good.

Assume nothing - Mixed media on paper, Photoshop 190 x 270 mm

Hot chips with vinegar

When I was ten

My best friend was a girl named Amy. On the weekends we would go roller-skating in the playground at our school or down my street. We sang in a children's choir and every Tuesday we would walk to the local primary school hall together for choir practice. On other afternoons we bought hot chips with vinegar, took them to the park and sat on the swings.

Sometimes we would climb the mountain at the top of my street and look at the sheep grazing in the valley on the other side. I loved to catch tadpoles, take them home and watch them turn into frogs.

My mother was busy (I suppose with five children she must have been), but my life was relatively quiet and uncomplicated. There were no computers and we weren't allowed to watch TV. After school and on weekends we played outside or at our friends' houses until it was dinnertime and after dinner we helped with the washing up and did our homework.

When I was twelve

Amy was still my best friend but I also played with another girl, Rebecca. I went to Rebecca's house most afternoons after school, as she lived nearby. Rebecca and I would hang around playing games (Monopoly) or cards (Go Fish) while she sucked sweetened condensed milk from a tube. This, together with a plate of biscuits was her afternoon tea. I was envious as I had never tasted condensed milk and my mother didn't allow us to have biscuits at home. We had milk, water and fruit at my house.

Sometimes when I knocked on Rebecca's door, her mother told me she wasn't at home. One day Amy took me aside and said that Rebecca's mother was lying when she told me that Rebecca wasn't home. According to Amy, Rebecca didn't like playing with me but she didn't want to tell me herself.

Apparently Rebecca would hide in the hallway or in the kitchen and get her mother to tell me she wasn't home. She would then stand behind the curtains looking at me through the window as I walked away. I knew Amy was telling the truth the day I saw Rebecca watching me from her bedroom window. I was shocked. Mothers didn't lie for their children. Did they? Mine wouldn't have, that's for sure.

I should have realised there and then that Rebecca was a bit weird. Who sucks condensed milk from a tube and hides in hallways so they don't have to see their friends? In her defence, she was shy and I did go to her house almost every day. Nevertheless …

I felt a burning sense of shame, embarrassment and humiliation. I believed that there must be something wrong with me if people who I thought were my friends didn't actually like me.

I kept these feelings close to my heart and spoke of them to no one. I stopped going out to play. I stopped roller skating, stopped climbing the mountain, stopped looking at the sheep and stopped catching tadpoles and watching them turn into frogs.

Amy and I didn't walk together to the park or to choir practice anymore and we didn't eat hot chips on the swings. I wondered if *anyone* liked me.

What if everyone was pretending, like Rebecca had been? I was no longer happy and carefree and I began to feel rather strange.

One day I realised I couldn't look people in the eye and it felt weird not to be able to do that. I wanted to. I tried and tried but I couldn't. It was like a hole in a tooth that you keep putting your tongue in to check if it is still there. It *was* there for what seemed like an awfully long time.

When I was fourteen

Mum was talking. I wasn't listening, I was thinking:

I don't want to die, but what if ...

... what if I topple from a tall building? What if I fall in front of a bus?

What if I am driving along the highway and I open the car door for some reason and roll out onto the road? If that happens, I hope I die straight away. I don't want to end up alive but all mangled or a vegetable. It won't be my fault. Honestly it won't. I don't want it to happen, really I don't.

So why is it, that when I am in the car, I get this weird feeling? This overwhelming sense that it's going to happen. It will be me doing it, but someone or someone else will be directing the action, making it happen.

Is it a premonition? Will it really happen? I don't want it to.

I tried not to think about it, but the scene played itself over and over in my mind: opening the car door, taking off my seatbelt and rolling out onto the road.

Splat.

I shuddered and crossed my arms quickly, mentally pushing down the button to lock the car door, checking my seatbelt, holding onto it tightly, then seeing ... the car door opening ... and rolling onto the road ... splat ... dead ... or maimed.

No, no, no ...

Mum looked at me expectantly, obviously waiting for a

response to something she had said.

'What?' I said, dragging my thoughts back to the present. 'WHAT?'

When I was fifteen

To all intents and purposes I was a normal teenager, and superficially I functioned normally. I ate meals with the family, did what I was told, went to school, completed all my homework and worked at my part time job.

I went through the motions, but I felt dead inside. I was numb. A glass wall surrounded me. There was no way in and no way out.

I felt nothing, not happiness, sadness or anger. Not pleasure or pain. Not love or hate. I was adrift. Isolated and desolate. I never cried and I never felt overtly sad or depressed, but I withdrew socially. I was totally disconnected from everyone and everything.

It was severe and unrelenting and I suffered terribly because of it.

I thought I had done something to cause it, and that I deserved to feel this way. I believed I was being punished for things I had done wrong, for being a bad person. I didn't consider it might be depression and neither did anyone else.

My parents knew something was wrong and took me to see a social worker. He talked to me, but we never got below the surface.

My mother took me on a holiday to Bali to see if that would help. It was lovely, but I was still not right.

After about two years, for no apparent reason, the fog began to lift. Slowly the numbness went away, and my life became normal again. I was well and happy.

For the next thirty years I was fine but I always wondered what had happened to me when I was fifteen.

At the age of forty-five, when I was diagnosed with late onset bipolar disorder, I read a brilliant book called *An Unquiet Mind* by an American author and academic, Kay Redfield Jamison, who wrote about herself and the pain and despair that depression caused her when she was a teenager.

I was amazed by her story. She could have been talking about me. I finally understood what had happened to me when

I was fifteen. All the feelings she'd had, I'd experienced as well. The way she wrote about her teenage years and the course of her bipolar disorder struck a chord deep within me.

My feelings of disassociation and isolation, my belief that I didn't have any friends, my separation from others by an intangible barrier, my inability to look people in the eye, my feelings of guilty and my reluctance to socialise suddenly made sense.

What had happened to me hadn't been something I had made up or done to myself. It hadn't been my fault. I was not the only one to have experienced it. Many other teenagers had (and still do). It had a name. Depression.

When I was seventeen

Life was good. I did all the things that normal seventeen year-old girls at that time did (which was nothing much). I had permed hair and wore flared jeans and satin blouses. I listened to ABBA and Rod Stewart. I was average academically at school and had some nice friends.

I worked part-time in a small supermarket and I loved being on the till, counting out the change and packing the groceries neatly into paper carry bags.

One Easter weekend my friend Melissa and I were on holidays at the South Coast with our respective families. She and her boyfriend were going out with his best mate and she asked if I wanted to go with them.

I met her boyfriend's mate and he was nice. I remember thinking at the time that he looked pretty good with his shoulder-length hair and brown eyes, dressed to kill in flared jeans, a tight light-blue collared body shirt and desert boots.

When I was twenty-one

I was married. My wedding day was perfect. My new husband and I beamed at each other throughout the church service. Melissa was my bridesmaid and her boyfriend was the best man. The children's choir sang beautifully. It rained as we came out of the church, a sure sign of good luck. I had everything I'd ever wanted and was blissfully happy.

Rainy Days - Oil on board 380 x 500 mm

The perfect mother

'Insanity is inherited – you get it from your children.' (Samuel Levenson)

I didn't go mad because I had children (although some women suffer terribly from post-natal depression). For me, the madness came much, much later.

All parents go a little stir crazy from time to time and I was no exception. Parenthood is hard. I had a few challenging times when my children were young (as we all do), but I was never really crazy. In fact, for a while, I was the perfect mother (or tried to be anyway).

Baby M

I had always wanted to have children, and when I became pregnant with Baby M, I was really excited. I read all the books and went to all the classes and prepared myself as best I could. I was determined to be the perfect mother. Baby M was fed according to a strict routine. Other people could nurse her, but no one could settle her or look after her as well as I could. My mother was given copious pages of notes about what to do if I had to go to an appointment and she was babysitting. I gave her no credit for having successfully raised five children of her own.

Baby M wore cloth nappies because it was so much better for the environment. When she dropped her dummy I picked it up, boiled it in water for ten minutes, then sterilised it in a special solution. She was introduced to solid foods in the exact order and timing suggested by the baby health clinic.

I cooked all of her food and put the excess into small Tupperware containers for when we went out. I bought fresh fruit and vegetables, chopped, peeled and gently boiled them, then mashed them into the perfect consistency.

As she got older, she never ate junk food, or drank soft drink or went to McDonald's. I read to her and talked to her, stimulating her brain to allow her intellectual potential to develop. I signed her up for baby swimming classes, baby music lessons and kinder gym activities.

I started toilet training her when she was one, and became very frustrated at her apparent lack of progress, compared to the boy next door.

I recorded every exciting detail of her progress and took albums full of photos. I wrote down what her first words were and when she said them and how tall she was at frequent intervals. Not only was she beautiful but she was very bright for her age.

Baby A

When Baby M was twenty months old, Baby A arrived. Another beautiful daughter. Of course I didn't have as much time as before but I still managed to cook the fruit and vegetables and wash the cloth nappies (double the quantities now as the toilet training with Baby M hadn't gone quite as I had planned). When Baby A dropped her dummy, I sat it in a cup of boiling water for a few minutes.

I couldn't give Baby A as much attention as I had given Baby M, which meant that if she cried for a little while, she was usually asleep by the time I finished what I was doing to attend to her. I couldn't understand why Baby M was such a bad sleeper and Baby A was such a good one.

My life was going according to plan and I was happy and content. I was raising my two small daughters, one with big hazel eyes, a happy smile and brown curls, and the other one with pale blue eyes, straight blonde hair and an easy-going personality. They complemented each other beautifully and life was good.

When my girls were four and two, my husband and I decided to have another baby. I wanted a boy this time, but told myself it didn't really matter as long as it was healthy.

We lived in the same street as a place called Sylvanvale. I had a vague idea it was some kind of educational institution, special school or sheltered workshop for 'mentally retarded' (as I thought of them) young people and adults. I didn't really know much about it and, to be truthful, didn't really want to know.

One day I was sitting on my front lawn, playing with my daughters and chatting to my next-door neighbour. A group of young adults from Sylvanvale approached with their carer. It appeared that they were learning how to cross the road. It wasn't a very realistic setting though, as we lived in a cul-de-sac and there was very little danger that any of them would be hit by a car.

I observed the group more closely thinking how awful it would be to have a child like that. Any other disability would be better than an intellectual one. A sensory impairment such as vision or hearing loss wouldn't be too terrible. Spina bifida or cerebral palsy couldn't be that difficult.

I could even cope with a child who had a life threatening illness. But having a child who was 'mentally retarded' was something I knew I simply could never deal with. It was a hypothetical train of thought anyway, as it was incomprehensible that any of these things could touch my life.

Preconceptions - Watercolour on paper 690 x 690 mm

Baby J

I felt such a sense of exhilaration. I had secretly wanted a son this time and after nine long months of waiting he had arrived. My husband and I were extremely pleased with ourselves and thought we had really been rather clever. Two gorgeous daughters and now a beautiful baby boy. The perfect family.

The delivery had gone well and although initially he had been a little blue and floppy the doctor told us that our baby was fine. He had been taken to the special care nursery for observation which the nurses assured us was routine. 'Nothing at all to worry about,' they said.

At midnight I should have been tired. My husband had gone home to ring our families and close friends to tell them the exciting news. I was back in my room, but couldn't sleep because the woman in the bed next to me was snoring loudly. I tried to read a magazine but couldn't concentrate. The post-natal hormones had kicked in and I was wide awake and feeling on top of the world. I decided to go back to the nursery and spend time with my new baby, rather than lie awake listening to a stranger snoring her head off.

The nightly hospital routines and activities went on around me. Beepers buzzed from time to time and whispered conversations drifted over me. At one stage I vaguely heard the nurses discussing another baby: 'The doctors have to check this one carefully. His head is very big and he has an older brother with Down syndrome.'

I looked over and compared my baby to the one with the big head. It was true, that baby really did have a big head. How ugly he was, I thought. And how perfect my baby was, with his fine features, rosebud mouth, cute little nose and gorgeous light brown hair. Just perfect.

As my newborn son slept I studied him carefully, taking in every tiny detail. I observed with interest that his eyes were quite far apart, the bridge of his nose was very flat, and that the tops of his ears were folded over. I thought it was amazing what the birth process did to babies, squashing their faces and heads out of shape like that.

Morning came and with it a visit from the residents and interns. They gathered around the end of my bed.

'The nurses said you stayed with your baby all night. Are you worried about him?' one of them asked.

'No,' I replied. 'He looks a little bit Chinese (I smiled) and his eyes are quite far apart, but I'm sure you will tell me he is fine and there is nothing to worry about.' I honestly had no idea.

They wrote notes on their clipboards and moved to the next bed.

I went back to the nursery and saw my baby being carefully examined by a young female doctor. I noticed that she looked extremely upset and her hands were shaking as she studied the bottoms of my baby's feet.

Instinctively I felt there was something seriously wrong, although I had absolutely no idea what it was. I looked over the doctor's shoulder at his feet and couldn't imagine what was causing her to react in such a disturbing way.

'What's wrong?' I asked.

The doctor hesitated and took a deep breath. She turned, looked at me, and said, 'I think your baby has Down syndrome.'

I'd had no premonition that anything was wrong. No warning. Surely I would have had some idea if there were a serious problem. It was unbelievable. The shock hit me. My stomach lurched, my body became numb and heavy, and my mind blurred. I felt strangely detached from my surroundings. I knew what Down syndrome meant, and how serious it was.

'But I'm only twenty-seven,' I said in disbelief, 'I'm too young.'

The doctor must have responded, but her voice faded away and I didn't take in anything else she said. I picked up my beautiful baby and took him into the next room to feed and comfort him.

I felt so sorry for him. It wasn't fair. Intense feelings of protectiveness washed over me. I decided to have at least ten more children so he would be surrounded by lots of brothers and sisters in a loving family environment. I tried to imagine having an intellectually disabled twenty year-old and thought about having the responsibility and burden of this child for the rest of my life. I cried and cried. I experienced a sense of total denial because this kind of thing just didn't happen to people like me. It happened to nameless, faceless people in women's magazines or on current affairs shows. It happened to other people.

I put Baby J back in the crib in the special care nursery and walked slowly back to my room. There was a new woman in the bed beside the door. It was the mother of the baby with the big head. It must have been obvious to her that something was wrong with me.

'Are you all right?' she asked.

'They think my baby has Down syndrome,' I blurted out.

'Oh,' she said. 'That's OK. My five year-old has Down syndrome.'

That meeting was to have a huge influence on my acceptance of and love for my son. I wondered if it was more than coincidence that we were both in the same hospital having babies at the same time. I came to believe that she was there was to teach me the things I needed to know about having a child with Down syndrome, and to help me understand the purpose of this part of my life's journey.

My husband would be coming in soon. How could I tell him? I didn't think I could say the words out loud. When he arrived I looked at him with concern, knowing I was about to shatter his hopes and dreams for his much loved son. I waited for a few minutes and then forced out the words.

'They think our baby has Down syndrome.'

He was stunned. I asked him to tell all our friends and relatives. I thought I could cope if people knew when they came in to visit, but there was no way I could tell them myself. He went home to ring everyone again. It was one of the hardest things he had to do in his whole life.

'You know I told you the baby is fine. Well actually, he has Down syndrome.'

It was incredibly painful for him, especially the call to his parents.

'Down syndrome, Mum … you know … it used to be called Mongolism … intellectually disabled … mentally retarded, Mum.'

It distressed him so much because he knew they didn't understand at all. He didn't really understand either. How could this have happened?

Back at the hospital I was desperate to see my daughters. They were four and two and my mum was with them. I rang my mum.

'Can you bring the girls to the hospital?'

'Is everything OK?' Mum asked.

I chose my next words very carefully.

'There is a problem with the baby. He is fine but there is a problem.'

I knew that Mum would find the news extremely upsetting and didn't want her to have a car accident on the way to the hospital.

A friend, who worked in the hospital and was on duty that day, popped in during a break. When I saw her I burst into tears again. A nurse came down and said I was to have a private room so my friend helped me load my belongings onto the bed. We both felt awkward and embarrassed as we made our way slowly down the corridor. I couldn't stop crying.

'It's not that I'm upset about him,' I said through my tears. 'It's just the shock, it's just the shock.' I said it over and over, probably to convince myself as much as my friend.

Rachel, the mother of the baby with the big head and the five year-old with Down syndrome, came to my room every evening and sat with me. I had so many questions for her. I had no idea how to react.

'How am I supposed to feel? How do I handle this? What do I even think about it?'

Rachel told me that she had cried every day for at least the first year of her son's life. 'I wasted all that time when I should have been enjoying my baby. People will react the same way you do. If you are devastated and believe it is the worst thing that will ever happen to you, then your visitors will be extremely upset and very sympathetic. If, on the other hand, you are cheerful and say something like 'Here, have a cuddle. Isn't he beautiful?' then people will be supportive in a more positive way, and they will take their cues from you.'

The idea that people's reactions could completely depend on my own response was a revelation to me. I tried being positive and was amazed by the results. Visitors would cautiously poke their heads through the door and look at me with a mix of concern and fear as if suddenly I had grown two heads. I would smile at them, invite them in and show off my beautiful baby boy. The visitors always relaxed, although some did make some stupid and insensitive comments.

'I'm glad it's not me,' said one close friend 'I just wouldn't cope at all.'

Comments like that really annoyed me, although in time I forgave my friends because I knew deep down they meant well. When they said things like this, I wanted to ask them, 'What would you do? Leave the baby in the hospital and forget he had been born? He didn't ask to have Down syndrome. It's not his fault.'

Still, they had come to visit, and I was very pleased to see them.

The people who really upset me were the friends who ignored his birth all together because they 'didn't know what to say or do'. From this experience I learned something about life. When bad or upsetting things happen to people it is important to visit, call or write, let them talk to you about what has happened, tell them you are thinking of them and offer support in small, practical ways. Ignoring them and pretending it didn't happen never makes you, or them, feel any better. If the person knows you are genuine and sincere they will be grateful for the efforts you make and overlook the awkward, upsetting, stupid or insensitive things you say.

This was one of those times in my life when something bad and upsetting had happened to me. I hadn't, and wouldn't have chosen to have a child with a disability (particularly an intellectual disability), but it had happened anyway. There were many ways I could choose to deal with it. I could spend my life feeling guilty, ashamed, embarrassed and sorry for myself, but I decided to love and accept him just as I loved and accepted my other children. How could I not? I had fallen in love with him even before he was born.

Baby T

My eldest daughter was just about to turn six, my second daughter was four, my toddler with Down syndrome was two and my youngest son, Baby T, had just arrived.

When his dummy fell out I wiped it on something, or sucked it, and then put it back into his mouth. Of course he didn't have cloth nappies, and home cooked meals were not often on the menu. I justified it on the basis that frozen, tinned and boxed food was really quite good, not all that different from the home made stuff, just more convenient.

There were no music, swimming or gymnastic lessons for him as a baby. He didn't miss out though, these things waited until he was five or six, an age he was developmentally ready to learn the skills.

As for child minding, I put him in occasional care (along with his sisters and brother) as often as I could afford to. Any offers from my mother, my sister, friends or neighbours were gratefully accepted. I never had time to leave them written instructions. A phone number was all they really need.

After four pregnancies in under six years, I struggled to get out of my maternity clothes and into normal clothes but by now my maternity clothes were my normal clothes. For quite a few years I didn't wear anything other than a tracksuit.

Baby T was much too young to eat solids, but he did have his first trip to McDonald's at six days old (his sister's birthday party). I had to remind myself from time to time to take photos of him, as months passed without me thinking of it. But he didn't miss out on much and he has learned that there are many advantages to being the youngest.

Shells - Pencil on paper 140 x 210 mm

Flux

I was happy at home raising my children and my youngest was now in preschool. Everything was fine but with four children and one income money was extremely tight. I had never taught on a permanent basis and didn't really want to return to teaching.

I wondered what else I could do and I tried working in a clothes shop for a while. My Bachelor of Education was in the back of my mind and I came to the conclusion that I didn't want to waste those four years of study. I applied to do relief teaching and after a very stressful interview, my casual teaching card arrived in the mail.

On my first day of work I was terrified, but I bluffed my way through and survived. I was very proud of myself for facing my fears and actually doing it. I ended up teaching full time and a few years later I returned to university to get my master's degree.

With a busy husband, four children (one of whom had Down syndrome), a full-time job and part-time university study, I was extremely busy, but my mental health was fine. If ever there was a time that I would have tipped over the edge into the world of bipolar, this would have been it, but I didn't.

On the day of my second graduation, I held my head high and smiled and waved at my husband, four children, mother, father and brother as I walked across the stage to receive my master's degree. Afterwards we went out to dinner to celebrate and my brother gave me a beautiful burgundy fountain pen.

Twelve years at home had eroded my self-confidence but two years of study restored it. I had never believed that I was very intelligent, but on graduation day I secretly told myself I *was* clever after all and I had just proved it.

I could do anything and the world was my oyster. I was thirty-nine years old and felt good about myself in a way I never had before.

The world may have been my oyster, but that was also the time the ocean currents began to swell. Giant swirling masses of seawater deep below the surface were transporting heat and chemicals. Powerful deep-sea cyclones and whirling underbellies swept through me for a few months that year.

It happened again three years later, then two years after that, then one year after that, always in spring. Something was going on. It was beyond the bounds of my consciousness, but it was there, nonetheless.

It was something …

something I would not know the name of for a very long time.

Flow - Acrylic on canvas 700 x 1000 mm

Sensing danger

When I was young my father used to take me fishing. He taught me that some fish liked bait, some liked prawns, while others preferred lures, luminous, shiny, enticing lures.

I often wondered whether the fish sensed danger, as some seemed wary and others oblivious. If they did sense danger, at what point did they realize they were in trouble?

The fish didn't seem to notice the hook at first. I would wait patiently to feel the slight vibration, the quivering and then the tautness on the line.

When the hook was firmly lodged in its mouth, the fish would be pulled along by a force that would slacken every now and then, perhaps lulling it into the false sense of security that it was still in control, able to swim around as before.

Inevitably though, it would be reeled in, released from the hook, left to flop around on the ground, and then placed in an empty bucket to be stabbed, gutted and scaled.

Now, so many years later, unaware that bipolar was on the line, I was just like one of those fish. I was staring at the lure, and my fate was sealed.

It was pre-determined, pre-destined and pre-ordained.

Mental health problems were in my family, not that I knew it then. I was oblivious. I had no idea I was swimming in a muddy gene pool, moving rapidly from the shallows into the murky depths.

I drifted along until something interesting caught my eye.

Suddenly an enticing lure was right there in front of me, beckoning.

I hesitated, sensing danger, but it looked so nice that I closed my mouth around it and in that instant it was too late. It stuck in my throat but I didn't notice the hook at first.

For a while I was fine, the strange tension intense and electrifying.

I was being pulled along by a force that slackened every now and then, lulling me into the false sense of security that I was in control, that I could do what I wanted, go where I wanted and have what I wanted.

Then, ever so slowly I was pulled further and further away

from safety. I started to struggle and I sensed I was in big trouble.

That's when the hook really dug in.

Drowning, not waving

Alone in pristine waters, surrounded by unimaginable beauty, translucent fish shimmered through the dazzling sunlight.

The ocean was glinting and teeming with life. It was a kaleidoscope of brilliant colours: Azure, the bright blue of the sky on a sunny day; Cobalt, rich with possibility; Cerulean, the soft blue of heaven mixed with the blue green of daydreams; and sapphire, emerald and jade, precious colours of peace, inspiration and hope.

The warm, crystal clear waters, so bright and shiny on the surface, deferred to their richer facets in the depths. It was stunning.

I loved the water, I always had.

Suddenly though, I was being swept out of my depth, pulled further and further out, beyond the breakers into open waters.

I had been having problems on and off for a few years, problems too difficult and personal to talk about to anyone. They were (I now know) the types of problems common to people who have bipolar disorder.

These problems started to bother me more and more, so I sought the help of a psychologist. She didn't help, so I saw a second psychologist, and then a third. All to no avail. Months and years went by.

The problems came and went, becoming worse each time. I knew that something wasn't right. The conflicting emotions I felt were emotions I didn't want to feel, and the places I was being drawn to were places I didn't want to go.

My rational mind was fighting something. What? I didn't know. All I knew was that I was in danger and desperately seeking help.

I was in deep water, becoming tired, weak and increasingly vulnerable.

A perfect target.

Suddenly, something was circling. It nudged me, testing my vulnerability and putting me off balance. Alarm bells rang. Shock and panic set in. I had no way of getting out of the water and I was really out of my depth.

I was holding my breath, running out of air, drowning not waving, and the life guard was nowhere in sight.

The light - Oil on canvas 300 x 400 mm

Rising

The delights of amphetamines

I was mis-diagnosed at first.

'*ADHD*,' the psychologist suggested.

'*ADHD*,' the psychiatrist agreed.

'*ADHD*,' the ADHD Clinic confirmed in their report.

It didn't ring true (who gets diagnosed with ADHD at age forty-five?), but hey, whatever. Two of my children had ADHD, so why not me? Try these pills the psychiatrist said as he wrote me a prescription for Dexamphetamine.

Dexamphetamine, or Dex, is a central nervous system stimulant whose actions resemble those of adrenaline, one of the body's natural hormones.

Dex was introduced in the 1930s as a remedy for nasal congestion, later used to treat ADHD, narcolepsy, obesity and depression.

Amphetamines are taken illicitly by some people seeking to experience the delights of their stimulating and euphoric effects. However, when taken for medical reasons by people with AHDH, they have a paradoxical, calming effect on the nervous system, which facilitates improved attention and concentration.

Having observed the calming effect on my children I assumed it would have the same effect on me.

Wrong.

I wasn't calm, I was energized, as if someone had plugged me into an electricity socket and switched me on.

Speed, bennies, glass, crystal, and uppers they are known as on the streets but there was no need of nightclubs or dodgy drug dealers furtively handing out pills for me. No, I only had to front up at the chemist with my script.

I'd never taken illicit drugs previously so I didn't know how taking amphetamines would make me feel. I can tell you now though, what taking Dex was like. On Dex I felt great, in fact better than great.

I could concentrate, I lost my appetite, lost weight and had plenty of energy. I had a sparkling personality and great wit (at least I thought I did). I bought size ten jeans and wore figure-hugging dresses. There was a sparkle in my eye. I felt a million dollars and looked it too (at least I thought I did).

Then there was the sex. I will say no more about the sex other than this … its no wonder people take party drugs. Anyway, naturally, that much fun could only last so long.

Fortunately, or unfortunately, it turned out that I didn't have ADHD and for me the stimulant effect of taking Dex was like lighting a match, starting the fire of hypomania, fanning the flames, creating a blaze and igniting a bushfire.

Nothing could extinguish it. It just had to burn itself out. Once the fire takes hold it's almost impossible to get it under control. 'Kindling' is what they call this effect in people with untreated bipolar disorder who take amphetamines.

Of course I shouldn't have been prescribed Dex, but how was I supposed to know? Still, it was the most creative, passionate and exhilarating time of my life, and while lots about it was very, very bad, I don't regret it one little bit.

The upward climb leaves you breathless.

Up, up, up you go and the view from the top of the mountain is magnificent. But, at some point, you start hallucinating because of the lack of oxygen, the blurring of your vision and fatigue, and when you reach the summit, the only way from there is down.

Free fall.

Maelstrom - Multimedia on cardboard 400 x 600 mm

A frenzy of photocopying

It didn't start with the photocopying but looking back that was one of the more flamboyant signs. I was planning a party for my son J's 18th birthday and decided it would be very creative to display large photographs of him in a continuous border at eye height around the room.

I chose the photos I wanted and took them to work. Every day after my colleagues had gone home I enlarged, copied and laminated 200 photos in a frenzy of photocopying.

I sent invitations to famous people. J's idols: Rowan Atkinson, Jerry Springer, The Rock and Pierce Brosnan. I was quietly confident that at least one of them would come and was very disappointed that none of them replied (I was especially disappointed about Pierce). Jerry Springer did send a t-shirt though, which was most exciting.

Other warning signs of my approaching mania were difficulty falling asleep, racing thoughts, increased activity, increased productivity, energy and rate of speech, talking over the top of people, spending sprees, heightened libido and irritability. It wasn't all bad; in fact, most of it was really fun. Who wouldn't want to have increased activity, productivity and energy? Not to mention incredible, mind blowing sex.

I would wait until the children went to bed, then do the folding and the ironing, put a few loads of washing into the machine, hang a few on the line (in the dark), tidy the house and mop the floor. Then I would go to bed, but not be able to sleep, so I would get up again, go to the computer and log on. I would google, e-mail and write for hours. When I would look up, it would be midnight, then three am and then four.

I would force myself to go to back to bed, not because I was tired, far from it, but because I had to get up at six to get the kids off to school and to then go to work. It was strange. After weeks of this I should have been exhausted, but quite the opposite, I had energy to burn. As my mania gathered momentum the early warning signs intensified and additional ones emerged. Obsessiveness, indiscretion, unusual and inappropriate behavior, risk taking and irrational thinking.

My birthday was approaching and my husband asked what I wanted for a present. I said I wanted a lime green Holden Monaro and if I couldn't have that then I wanted a tattoo. A big one with beautiful flames of red, orange and yellow, flaring up my right arm from my elbow to my shoulder. My husband assumed I was joking but I wasn't. I was deadly serious.

He said 'no' to the Monaro and 'NO' to the tattoo. It didn't matter. I knew I could talk him around, if not about the car, then definitely about the tattoo. I had made up my mind. It wouldn't matter what he said. Anyway with my increased energy, enthusiasm and libido he found it difficult to deny me anything.

Recognising the warning signs of approaching mania means there can be earlier and more effective treatment through harm minimization, self-management, awareness, understanding, communication, reassurance and relapse prevention. An action plan can also be developed. That's all well and good if you know what's going on, which of course I didn't.

When your mood is stable you usually have regular

appetites, sleep patterns and energy levels. You have reasonable decision-making skills, planning and organisational abilities.

Your actions and reactions are appropriate. You feel comfortable with yourself, in your own company and with others. You don't have obsessive thoughts and, in fact, you are usually not even aware of the state of your mood at all.

When you are manic you usually don't sleep for more than a few hours a night. Sleep problems are both cause and effect of unstable bipolar. You are irritable, hyperactive and restless. You can be angry and aggressive. Your behavior is disinhibited and impulsive. You spend money, lots of money, buying multiples of things that are expensive, things you don't need. You argue persuasively and passionately rationalise every decision you make and every action you take.

When I was manic I said,

'Of course I'm not manic. I am fine. In fact I'm better than fine. I feel fantastic.'

When I was manic I thought,

'There's absolutely nothing wrong with me. I'm not ill. This medication is going in the bin.'

When I was manic I couldn't stop moving, sit still, slow down, relax, watch TV, or read a magazine or a book.

When I was manic, I appeared articulate and coherent, logical, organized, persuasive and determined. I could fool anyone, even myself.

Especially myself.

The life model - Charcoal on paper 430 x 600 mm

29

Before the trouble came the fun

I pushed open the heavy glass doors and stepped over the threshold. I smiled and we hugged. I panicked to think I had turned up unannounced, but no, I was expected after all. However important this visit, a casual air was fundamental to the process.

Ours was a unique relationship. We had been seeing each other for six years.

James loved women. All types of women. Plain women and beautiful women. He charmed them all as he charmed me, seduced them as he seduced me. I was a testament to the futility of resistance.

I offered myself up to him, time and time again, unable to break away. After I had been with him I felt different. People noticed. Pleasure lingered.

Before James, I had been with others. When it didn't work out, I would hide myself away. It always took me so long to get over a bad experience. What was done was done. I would search for someone new, someone who wouldn't ride roughshod over me, ignoring my hopes and dreams and my expressed desires. Each time I would move forward, searching for someone I could trust.

Someone like James.

Contact between James and I, of course, had established non-negotiable boundaries and it was risky telling him my fantasies.

'Hi,' he said, 'it's lovely to see you.' He smiled and lightly touched my arm.

'It's good to see you too.' I replied. His hair was different, but he looked as gorgeous as ever.

James placed his hand on the small of my back, and guided me across the room.

I smiled too, anticipating the pleasure he would give me over the next few precious hours, the time I had stolen from other things, and other people. I had been looking forward to this for so long.

The black leather lounge beckoned and I relaxed into its soft contours. I felt a weakening in my limbs as I surrendered to his touch. I basked in the sensations, the heat, the warmth and the familiar scent.

I had finally arrived at my holiday destination. As James massaged my aching temples, the ocean murmured and the waves lapped on a summer shore. I could hear the sound of my heart beating and feel the warmth of the sun on my skin.

I had known it would be like this, it always was. I abandoned myself to the ecstasy and the sensuality, but all too soon, James roused me from my dreams. He took me by the hand, pulled me gently to my feet, and led me to a chair on the other side of the room.

I sat down and waited.

James looked at me intently, without speaking. It is an acquired skill, the art of concentration. No words were needed. We had known each other too long.

I trusted James completely. He could do anything and I would let him.

We both knew it.

Defiantly trying to resist all attempts to think, I closed my eyes. When I opened them again, he was still looking at me, debating and deciding.

He rested his hands lightly on my shoulders, and then ran his fingers through my hair, tilting his head to one side and raising an eyebrow. He moved closer still. I could feel his warm breath on my neck, my cheek, my ear and my shoulder.

'Sit still,' I said to myself. 'Relax.'

I knew it was my pleasure that drove him, my happiness that satisfied him.

I had been there for hours, but finally it was time to go. I tried not to feel guilty about the time I had spent with him, and what I knew it would cost me. James played with my hair and smiled. He told me I looked beautiful, and then he kissed me on the cheek.

'Thank you,' I said, my eyes shining. 'I love it, I really love it.'

I smiled at James as I handed my credit card to the girl behind the desk at my favourite hairdressing salon.

Things were looking up.

Before I was hypomanic, going to the hairdresser was a nice, but ordinary activity. When I was hypomanic nothing was ordinary. My senses were heightened and I experienced sounds, shapes, colours, textures, tastes and scents much more vividly than ever before in my life.

James is still as gorgeous as ever, but sadly, having him cut my hair is now an ordinary experience once again. My medication sees to that.

I miss the sensuality of hypomania so much. My life is so bland without it. My psychiatrist tells me, 'It's not bland, it's normal', but I know it's really bland. 'Normal' is not all it's cracked up to be.

It's why some people refuse to take their medication.

My career as a world-class ice skating champion

People who know me might be surprised to learn that a few years ago I had a secret life as an aspiring ice skating champion. I kept it quiet, not wanting to 'big note' myself.

I was (unknowingly) hypomanic and enjoying life immensely. I had a great idea, why not take up ice-skating?

I went to the local ice rink and signed up for classes, three a week. I embraced this new adventure with excitement and delight. I knew it would be great.

I started my lessons and loved them. It was amazing. As the weeks flew by, my skills improved in leaps and bounds. I learned to skate forwards, backwards, in circles and with one foot crossing over the other. I danced (once) with a partner. I loved it with a passion, until the day my dream was shattered.

I got my ambitions mixed up with my capabilities and had a serious altercation with the barrier, followed closely by the hard, unyielding ice. My back took the brunt of the fall.

I lay on the ice in pain and shock. I couldn't move, but no-one seemed to notice and no-one came over to help me. Eventually I crawled to the barrier on my hands and knees and lay on the timber seats for the longest time before being able to get up and make my way home.

That was the end of that. My career as an ice skating champion was over. In the face of injury, I turned to other less physical pursuits. Painting and drawing. Writing.

I look back on my ice skating career with pride.

I was so good, so good.

Well, I could have been.

Hypomania had convinced me of that.

My life as a Ferrari

If I was a car, I'd be a Ferrari. A red one, of course.

Red. That incomparable colour, unique to Ferraris, against which all other car colours are judged. A gleaming sports car with a twelve-cylinder engine.

As a Ferrari, I am a member of an exclusive club and when I meet other Ferraris we recognise each other instantly. Each of us is unique but we have a great deal in common.

We can go from 0 to 60 in 4.3 seconds and the faster we go, the louder we sound. The manufacturers of other cars try to mute the noise of their engines, but not Ferrari. We spring to life with a roar that is exhilarating, one that resonates with the sound of distant thunder.

However, as beautiful, powerful and distinctive as we are, we can be unreliable and unpredictable at times. We start out well, but our engines make strange noises and ominous sounds come from within. We can break down completely and end up in the pits.

I require more than the average amount of maintenance and parts are expensive and hard to come by. You shouldn't leave me alone in the car park even to just duck into the shops. To repair me after the smallest scrape costs almost as much as I am worth.

When the key turns and I refuse to come to life, people try to convince me to change. Wouldn't it be easier to be a safer or more reliable type of vehicle?

I try to convince myself too, but ultimately, I don't want to change. There is a lot to like about being a Ferrari. Besides I have joined roadside assistance and become good friends with my local tow truck driver.

Yes, I might break down sometimes and yes, I am expensive to maintain, but when I am firing on all cylinders, I am spectacular. I have a confidence and energy that everyone admires and envies.

As a Ferrari, I don't care about breaking down and I don't care if I crash and burn.

I enjoy the exhilaration while it lasts.

Crash and burn - Oil on board 380 x 460 mm

The silken web

I was drawn to the silken web

The spider sat motionless
watching me
mesmerising me
with its sickening beauty

I was lulled by the soft
sensual feel of the flimsy fibres

My fingers hovered
above the gossamer threads
then rested momentarily

Only then did I feel the danger
and understand the predicament
that I was in

I could not pull away
and leave it untouched

Once two things have bonded
you cannot prise them apart
without damaging or destroying
one or the other

or both

Have you ever really looked at a spider's web? Seen the symmetrical patterns of silk, bejeweled with dew, glistening in the early morning light?

Have you ever really looked at a spider? You might think spiders are ugly, but I have seen beautiful ones too (in books). Exotic tarantulas with bodies of cobalt blue and lime green, hairs that are blood red and bright orange, and toes in hues of pinks and purples.

Spiders are predators, dangerous and deadly. Some spiders hunt and others fish. They use stealth to avoid detection and then ambush their prey. Other spiders simply sit and wait for something tantalising to cross their path.

Spiders kill by biting. The bite contains venom that dissolves the insides of the prey, and once it has taken effect, the spider literally sucks it dry.

Some people are like spiders, beautiful and charismatic on the outside. They hunt or just sit and wait until someone strays into their line of sight. They recognise potential prey in the blink of an eye and then single-mindedly and stealthily pursue it. They suck you in, and then bleed you dry, leaving your life in tatters. Once they have finished with you they just set their sights on someone else.

It's not personal.

If you've been bitten, you will know this to be true.

Once bitten, twice shy.

I hate spiders.

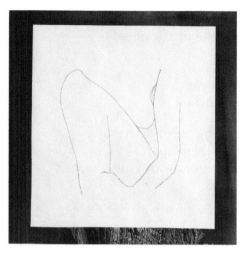

Exposed - Pencil on paper 300 x 400 mm

The Ferndale Ladies Erotica Society

Joanne and I met at a community college writing course. Every week the teacher would ask us to write a story in a particular genre, and then someone would be chosen to read theirs out loud to the group. It was all pretty straightforward until the week we were asked to write an erotic short story.

This was a challenge as none of us had ever read much erotica, let alone written any, but we took on the challenge as only a group of middle-aged suburban women could. When Joanne read her erotic story out loud the rest of us were astonished. It was good, very good. We all started thinking.

When the course finished, we decided to continue meeting each week at Joanne's house in Ferndale Street, to write erotica together and publish a book of our collected short stories.

After our first meeting we agreed that each of us would bring a completed erotic short story to the next meeting. I went to the local bookshop and was amazed at the selection. I chose a book and started reading, beginning to think this might not be my cup of tea after all.

My first problem was what to write about and my second was how to start. I kept putting it off, finding more 'important' things to do. What I needed was inspiration.

A few days later, I was at a three-day work conference. It was after lunch on the second day and everyone was yawning.

Although the topic was interesting, and relevant to my work, the presenter used too much jargon, and spoke in sentences so long, his train of thought was extremely difficult to follow. It was going to be a very long afternoon. Still, it wasn't all bad. Ben had followed me in and was now sitting beside me.

Ben was friendly and down to earth, which made a nice change from some of my other colleagues, who had an arrogant air about them. They were academic doctors in ivory towers unlike Ben, who was a doctor too, but a medical one. Ben was fun.

For the most part we watched attentively, listened carefully and behaved with decorum, but the lecture was so tedious it was difficult to stay focused. Ben glanced sideways at me and raised his left eyebrow ever so slightly. A conspiratorial smile and it was game on.

I took my conference program turned it over and drew a three by three grid. I placed a cross in one of the squares and pushed it towards Ben. We played noughts and crosses first, then boxes, and then we started writing notes to one another, making disparaging and witty comments about the presenter and the people around us.

After a while that got boring and Ben didn't appear to be in the mood to play games any more. He yawned, focusing back on the speaker. I tried to concentrate by taking lecture notes but it didn't help. The man on my other side was writing furiously. Without moving my head, I glanced across to see what he was writing about. It was a letter to a friend. I couldn't think of any friends to write to.

Then I had an idea. I folded down the top page of my note pad so it would cover my writing. I could move it down as I went, leaving exposed only the line I was working on. I looked around surreptitiously to see if anyone was watching me, then placed one arm over the paper and the other one across the desk, to provide a natural barrier between Ben and I. Perfect.

I was good at writing academic papers, but there isn't much erotica in academia. I wondered whether I had any of the prerequisite skills necessary to write in this particular genre.

Surely I could make something up. How hard could it be? I put pen to paper waiting for inspiration. When none came, I decided to start by just writing freely, a stream of consciousness.

After a slow start I began scribbling frenetically, making sure my work was covered at all times. A story was starting to take shape in my mind. Its structure must have all the conventional elements: a scene; characters; foreplay; conflict; climax and resolution.

The lecture continued ad nauseam. I looked at Ben and squinted, trying hard to imagine him in a different context, an erotic one. He was quite attractive. Wasn't he? Well ... no, not really. He was nice, but average looking. Nevertheless, he would have to do. I decided to model my protagonist on Ben and away I went.

After about three pages Ben leaned towards me and whispered,

'What are you doing?'

I didn't want to give him the wrong idea. Or did I? I was starting to have fun. What harm could a little mischievous flirting do?

I smiled, turned my head and whispered seductively in his ear.

'I'm writing erotica.'

Ben looked shocked. The lecture was hardly one to inspire writing at all, let alone that type of writing.

'Really?' he whispered back, an incredulous look on his face.

'Yes,' I said quietly.

'Really?' he said again.

'Yes Ben. Really.'

'Can I read it?' he asked.

'No, of course not,' I said. As if I would let him read it.

'I'll be your editor if you like,' he added, almost pleading.

'Thanks but no thanks,' I replied.

There was no way Ben was going to read my story. Professionally there are lines you shouldn't cross, and even though my judgment was significantly impaired at the time, I was well aware that this was one of them.

When the lecture finished I made sure I took the notes with me out to afternoon tea and kept them close.

'Are you sure you don't want me to be your editor? I could proof read your story tonight and give it back to you in the morning,' Ben asked one more time.

'Sure I'm sure, but thanks for offering,' I replied.

The next morning at 8.45am, Ben and I were both back for day three of the conference. Ben asked how my writing was coming along.

'Fine thanks,' I said.

He leaned towards me, lowering his voice and whispering something in my ear, so softly I had to strain to hear him. Something about going home the afternoon before and taking a cold shower. 'All that talk of erotica,' he added unnecessarily, by way of explanation.

I was amazed. Ben hadn't read one word of what I had written. It was simply the thought of it that had made him so excited.

I only wished I could have written what Ben thought I had written, whatever that might have been, but sadly, of course, it was impossible to ask him. Nevertheless, his reaction was most interesting.

Maybe there was going to be something in writing erotica after all. I couldn't wait to tell the girls at the next meeting of The Ferndale Ladies Erotica Society.

If I have one regret about my erotica writing days, it is this. Recently, a woman, who lived in the same suburb as Ferndale Street, published a book of erotica and made an absolute fortune.

It should have been me.

Nude - Charcoal on paper 460 x 590 mm

Through the eyes of a child

'Imperfection is beauty, madness is genius and it's better to be absolutely ridiculous than absolutely boring.' Marilyn Monroe

When you're hypomanic, creativity seeps through the pores of your skin and splashes onto the page, or the canvas, or whatever you are doing. I was writing a lot. Erotica, of course, academic papers and journal articles, short stories, fiction (albeit not very well) and poetry.

I decided to write a poem from the perspective of a young child. It could be the child of a parent who has a mental illness, but equally, it could be the child of a parent who does not.

My Mum's Mad

My mum's mad, she's crazy
and silly a lot of the time
I love her madly, truly
I love her because she's mine

My mum can be excitable
and also very loud
She talks and flaps her hands about
She stands out in a crowd

Once we put on our swimmers
and danced outside in the rain
We laughed and sang and jumped about
Dad said we were insane

When she's sick she stays in bed
she doesn't answer the phone
We can't go out to the park and play
we have to stay at home

We must be quiet some mornings
she doesn't like any noise
She doesn't speak, she talks with her hands
Shhh, play with your toys

She drives my dad to the bus stop
in her nightie and dressing gown

One day when we were driving home
Guess what? The car broke down

Sometimes when she is driving
she says a naughty word
She swears and points her finger
I pretend I haven't heard

Sometimes she looks dishevelled
I hate when people stare
My face goes red, hot and flushed
I wish I wasn't there

My mum washes her hands a lot
she always mops the floor
Before we go out she checks the lights
the oven and the door

At times she's neat and fussy
but then she's couldn't care less
Mum says nobody's perfect
who cares if the house is a mess

When dad brought home the man from work
Mum was in a rush
She threw everything in a cupboard
and told us all to hush

I drew on myself with texta once
Mum drew on herself too
hers did not come off in the bath
because hers is a tattoo

At times my mum is silly
but she's never ever mean
She tells me I'm a princess
and treats me like the queen

Some days she tells me stories
of magic and witches and then
we make shadow animals on the wall
and then bake gingerbread men

When I help my mum says thanks
'My goodness what a pleasure'
I heard her tell my grandma once
that I'm her little treasure

And when the world's too crazy
there's only one place that I want to be
Safe and warm and snuggled up
sitting on my mum's knee

Two hearts - Oil pastel and ink 80 x 270 mm

Other people's stories

While this book consists mostly of my stories, other people
with bipolar disorder have stories too. These are some of their
stories.

The philosophy of a person under the influence of mania is:

*Always surrender to temptation for it may never pass your way
again.*

I have spoken to people who have been manic and surrendered to all sorts of temptations.

Some have spent so much money that they have lost their homes. Some have slept with people they shouldn't have and become pregnant and/or lost their families because of it.

Some have driven way over the speed limit and crashed their cars, or been caught driving under the influence, once, twice or three times. Some have found God, or thought they themselves were God.

Often people are prescribed medication, which they take until they feel better. Then they stop taking it, because they do feel better. Then they start to become ill again, but cannot see that they are not well. Others can see what is happening, but it takes another significant episode for the person to get help and go back on their medication again. It can be a vicious cycle and with each episode they do more damage to themselves, to their reputations and to their relationships. The damage is often severe and irreparable.

Question: If you have bipolar disorder, and have been prescribed medication which you've decided not to take, what should you do?

Answer: Do not pass go. Do not collect $200 and go straight to the doctor.

It is very important to have confidence in your doctor and to see them regularly when you are unwell and occasionally when you are well. This is why. If you trust your doctor, and have a good relationship with them, you will be more likely to follow their advice at those times when your judgment is impaired.

I met a woman recently at a one-day seminar for people with bipolar disorder. She was clearly very manic, and in the lunch break told me how proud she was of herself that she had gone off her medication on the advice of her naturopath.

She argued most passionately and persuasively that her bipolar was under control and that a course of colonic irrigation had helped by removing toxins and impurities from her body. She said she had never felt better.

In the next breath (she had hardly paused for breath) she also told me about her run of recent bad luck and how she had lost her job, her husband and all her money in a failed business venture. She had no insight at all.

She pressed me to exchange contact details, as we had (according to her) 'connected' so well. I took her contact details but didn't offer her mine.

There are so many stories. If you had bipolar disorder you would have stories too. What would mania be like for you?

Hypothetical instructions for the simulation of mania.

Go to sleep at 3.00am and wake up at 6.00am again. You will have been doing this every day for a few weeks now. Don't waste time having breakfast, you won't be hungry. You won't need coffee either as you will have that lovely, buzzy feeling without it. Get dressed and race to work.

At the office, be energetic and enthusiastic. You know your clients love you and your boss does too (at least you think they do). Make sure you work through your lunch hour. Quick quick, hurry hurry.

Talk over the top of people, move quickly and think quickly. Hurry, but look calm on the outside. Do ten things at once. You're a machine on high speed. Sort, file and shred. Churn through the morning, leaving everyone and everything behind in your wake. Send everyone in the office some funny and clever e-mails. Surely no one will think that they are inflammatory, rude, sexist, lewd or indecent.

Take offence at those colleagues who are now looking at you strangely and talking about you behind your back. They've always had it in for you, you know they have. It will dawn on you that you've always hated your job and your boss. Maybe you should resign. Yes, that's a good idea. With your skills and experience it will be easy to get another one. Don't agonise about it, act decisively. Write out your resignation and go and find your boss. Tell him exactly what he can do with his job. Pack up your things and leave work straight away.

Now is the perfect time to go to the car dealership to look at the new red Ferrari you have had your eye on. Even though it's wildly expensive you will be able to afford it somehow. There's your severance pay, of course, and if that's not enough you can always get a loan. Sign the contract for the car on the spot, it will cheer you up.

On the way home, stop at the shops to get a few things, something to eat and a take away coffee. Rant at the man in the coffee shop because the coffee's too cold/strong/weak/ expensive. Yell at the girl in the mobile phone shop, who is trying to help you sort out what to do about the extremely expensive mobile phone you have lost.

When you get back in the car, drive over the speed limit, eat your hot chips and drink your coffee, while at the same time texting and weaving in and out of the peak hour traffic. Swear loudly at the really bad drivers, especially the ones who won't let you cut in. Bastards. Take a detour and stop at the local club for a little time to 'chill out' and celebrate your freedom and your red Ferrari. Then, put the contents of your bank account into a poker machine and have unprotected sex in the car park with someone you have just met at the club.

Intense thoughts, strong emotions and out of control feelings will be swirling around and around in your mind. Spinning faster and faster and faster and faster and faster and faster dragging you further and further under. Your judgment is severely impaired.

Everything is surreal. You know what you are doing, but you just don't know why. You are having a manic episode and it will cost you, and those who care about you, dearly.

The taste of chocolate

I live in a beautiful house
eat crumbs from the floor
then one day I see chocolate

I'm not stupid
I've seen others die in traps before
but I'm sure

I can get the chocolate without getting caught
My nose quivers
I weigh up the risk

Slowly I start to pull the chocolate from the trap
SNAP
the metal bar crashes down on my tail

It's excruciating
I have no choice
but to pull and strain

when my tail is gone
I scurry away
bleeding and sore

a part of myself gone
exchanged for promise of sweet pleasure
the taste of chocolate

Manic - Pencil on paper 100 x 200 mm

Cooking up a storm: recipes for disaster

Recipe #1 Mania

Main ingredients
1 teaspoon euphoria
2 tablespoons irritation
3 cups restlessness
1 cup grandiosity
1 dessertspoon psychosis (optional)
8 Virgin credit cards
6 various sex toys
3 large tattoos
4 adventurous business plans

Additional ingredients
Inappropriate (exciting) sexual activity
Gross (extravagant) overspending
Outrageous (energetic) behaviour
Drugs and alcohol (optional)
Unwavering drive
Determination
Inappropriate or public places

Cooking method
Add main ingredients together and mix on low speed in a blender at home, at work and in the car, with friends, relatives and strangers.

Sprinkle liberally with energy, enthusiasm, passion, creativity, sociability and spontaneity. Limit quantities of sleep and food.

Blend on medium speed for a few weeks or months, gradually increasing the speed to the highest setting. The ingredients will combine to form peaks of accelerated speech, impaired judgement and impulsive behavior.

Fold in any, or all, of the additional ingredients and stir enthusiastically. Bake in a pressure cooker in bright light and sunshine at an extremely high temperature. The mixture will rise rapidly and expand until fully cooked.

The icing on the cake
Blend obsessive thoughts with paranoia and spread generously

covering all areas. For a truly first class result dust with delusions and hallucinations.

Serving instructions
Serve at regular intervals throughout the day, week, month, season or year. If you are partial to this recipe spring is a good time to gorge yourself.

Warning
Ensure you monitor the temperature gauge on the crock-pot or pressure cooker. Never leave them unattended and always be vigilant, watching for early warning signs of an impending explosion.

Fire is a serious threat to health and safety and there is a real risk when cooking this recipe that your house will burn to the ground, badly injuring or killing not only yourself, but also those around you. A severe blaze will cause long-lasting pain and permanent disability, requiring rehabilitation and lifelong treatment. It is worth the expense of buying a fire extinguisher. Keep the contact number of the local fire brigade at hand. Use it if you need to and act early. Don't wait until it is too late and the fire has taken hold.

Recipe #2 Depression

Main ingredients
1 teaspoon sadness
2 tablespoons irritation
3 cups fatigue
1 cup guilt
1 dessertspoon social isolation (essential)
1 bed
1 lounge
Pyjamas or old clothes
Slippers and dressing gown (optional)

Additional ingredients
Lack of energy
Inability to think properly, make decisions or concentrate
Recurrent thoughts of death

Cooking method
Mix main ingredients together and put blender on low speed

by yourself at home. Sprinkle liberally with grief, pain, loss, anxiety and despair. Do not add pleasure, energy or happiness. Definitely do not add sex. Don't be concerned about the lack of these ingredients in your dish. You won't have a taste for them anyway. Blend on low speed for a few weeks or months. Do not increase the setting, if anything change it to a lower speed. The ingredients will combine to form a thick dough of depression, pessimism, doom and gloom.

Slowly fold in any or all of the additional ingredients and mix through. Bake in a crock-pot or slow cooker in a dark room for days, weeks, months or years. For some people this can take a lifetime. Do not expect the mixture to rise, even when it is fully cooked.

The icing on the cake

Blend quantities of irritability and self-loathing and spread generously. For a truly first class result, sprinkle despair over the top.

Serving instructions

Serve at regular intervals throughout the day, week, month, season or year. Winter is the best time to dish it up, if you can be bothered.

Self portrait - Oil on canvas 500 x 600 mm

Falling

The inescapable law of gravity

Step into the roller coaster and sit down. Strap yourself in. Remember, there are no controls. The roller coaster will start to creep up the slope, then the ground will inch away. It will gather potential energy as it is slowly pulled to the top. It will reach the summit, and then suddenly plummet. You will scream. The stored, potential energy will convert to kinetic energy as the roller coaster begins its stomach-churning descent. Gravity and friction will control the rest of the ride. Finally it will slow down, and come to a stop. You'll be stunned; your heart will still be racing. What a ride. Sit there and catch your breath. It won't be long until the ride begins again.

What goes up must come down. For every high there is an equal or greater low.

The worst thing is that there is no escape.

After the cycles happen once, twice and ten more times, you know it will happen again, and again. You just don't know when or why.

You can be vigilant and do all the right things, but depression will sneak up on you while you are not watching.

It will creep up behind you and stab you in the back.

Then, as you lie bleeding and look back in shock and horror, wondering how this could have happened again, you see the assassin in the shadows.

It is obvious now; he was there all the time. You just couldn't see him approaching.

Next time you will know though. Next time you will see him there, stalking you. You're sure you will. Only you won't. You'll recover. Life will be good again and your mood will stabilise. You'll be back to normal. You'll forget. You will.

The assassin will wait patiently in the shadows, biding his time. He will wait for the days to change, for the weeks to pass and the seasons to turn.

He will wait for nature to take its course. Then it will happen.

Again.

Falling - Multimedia 460 x 590 mm

Paying the piper

I'd had the mania and danced to the tune but now I was paying the piper. They say the higher you fly the further you'll fall. It's true. That's just the way it is. None of the words that follow can give a sense of what it was like to be clinically depressed, because there are no words to accurately describe how it is.

I couldn't do much. The only thing I could do was sleep. Every morning I would wake up and think,

'Not another day, another long, awful, agonising day that I have to somehow endure until it is time to close my eyes again.'

The only respite I had was when I was asleep and yet, during the day, I kept going, forcing myself to do the things I had to do.

I tried to keep it hidden but my ability to act normally could only last for a very brief time, if at all. The people I couldn't completely hide it from were my husband and my children.

I was tired, desperately, achingly tired, with absolutely no energy at all. My limbs were strangely heavy. I saw everything through a fog. Literally. I couldn't see properly. I was sure that there was something wrong with my eyes, even though two optometrists told me otherwise.

I couldn't make decisions about anything. What to do what to eat or what to wear. I would stand in front of my wardrobe, frozen, unable to choose something to wear, anything. I would stand in front of the fridge opening and closing the door. I would go to the shops and come home with nothing, having abandoned a half full trolley when it all overwhelmed me. Choices about anything were much too hard to make.

My husband would sit watching me, shaking his head, bemused, almost amused, but it wasn't funny. From my perspective, there wasn't anything to smile about.

Every single thing I had to do was impossibly difficult. I felt like I was climbing Mt Everest without oxygen. Easy routine tasks became impossible. I couldn't even decide what to have for dinner. I couldn't fathom how to summon the energy to take out a recipe book, look in the cupboard, write a list, get my keys and purse, get into the car, drive to the shops, find a parking spot, walk around the supermarket, find the things I needed, stand in the queue, take the things out of the trolley, pay the money, put the bags into the trolley, lift the bags out of the trolley, put the bags into the car, take the trolley back, drive home, and so on, and so on, so I didn't do it.

Everything was overwhelming, impossible and unrealistic. I couldn't fathom how other people managed to do these things. I couldn't read and I couldn't watch TV. The only thing I wanted to do was sleep and even that often eluded me. Yet I kept going on autopilot, moving through the quicksand that was my terrain, totally detached from it all and from everyone and everything. I knew with absolute certainty, that everything I did was pointless anyway. If I shopped and cooked today I would only have to turn around and do it again tomorrow. Why bother?

I forced myself to put one foot in front of the other though for what purpose I had no idea, other than the vague notion, somewhere in the recesses of my mind that I just had to do it. I had to while away my days one agonizing minute, one mind-numbing hour, one awful day at a time.

I had no memory of a time when my life wasn't like this. No memories of good things and no knowledge that there were ever, or could ever be, happy times. No recollection of the fun and energy of mania. I was in a vacuum, a purgatory of despair

The only thing that kept me from doing away with myself was the fact I had no energy to plan or carry out an attempt and perhaps the hazy notion that one day, maybe, by some miracle, things might not be this way.

Despite what people thought, no one could jolly me out of it, and no one could fix it. They tried to help but their questions were stupid and my answer to their questions was often 'NO!' I couldn't try any harder to get better and 'NO!' I couldn't control it. People really were stupid and insensitive. They meant well, I'm sure, when they told me that life wasn't meant to be easy. Idiots. As if I didn't know that life wasn't meant to be easy.

They said how much better off I was than this person or that situation. As if I cared about this person or that situation. They said if I hadn't been to see a psychiatrist in the first place none of this would have happened. As if I believed that. People really were that stupid and insensitive. They told me to exercise, think happy thoughts and do half an hour of exercise or yoga every morning. As if that would fix everything. People were dense and unsupportive. Fucking useless, or so I thought at the time.

A friend said, not unkindly, 'I'm surprised you have no resilience. Can't you control it?' She had no idea how hard I fought it, every step of the way, every second, every minute. I WAS resilient. I refused to give in to it but it overwhelmed me anyway. I tried to keep it hidden as much as I could but when the depression was at its worst, my ability to act normally could only last for a brief time.

I went in to work for half an hour one day and held it together. At least I thought I had until someone said later they thought I hadn't been quite myself. Another time I gave an hour's lecture at a national conference to about a hundred of my colleagues, presenting from notes I had miraculously prepared. I was articulate and coherent, so I am told, but I had no recognition of the words I was saying, no comprehension of the sentences and no memory afterwards of any of it.

What did feeling normal mean? Who knew? Certainly not me. I had no concept, no memories of a happy past and no hope for anything other than despair in my future. That's just the way it was.

Depression is elusive, a master of disguise. We all have preconceived notions and stereotypical views of what we think it might be. Some people do fit the stereotypes but a lot don't. Like me.

Even when I was severely depressed no one knew. Outwardly, I didn't present in a sick or needy or desperate fashion. I looked just the same as I always did, just the same as I look now. I think a lot of depressed people don't fit the stereotype, which is why suicide comes as such a shock.

My depression was as hard for my family as it was for me, or maybe harder.

My husband found it extremely difficult. When things were really bad, my psychiatrist told him (and explained to me in clear and unequivocal terms), that it was very important for him to retain some distance. I was very 'needy' and wanted to talk incessantly about what was happening to me. Bipolar disorder and my depression were the only things I could, or wanted to, talk about.

The doctor said that it was like I was drowning, pulling my husband down with me, and if things kept going the same way, we would both go under. If that happened, my husband wouldn't be able to work, and so on and so on. The way the doctor explained it to me was helpful. I stopped being so intense about it all and stopped going on and on about myself. My husband felt validated about having some emotional distance. Nevertheless, it was very stressful on our relationship.

My husband was wonderful. He didn't understand what I was going through, but he cared. He kept things normal as much as possible. He accepted the fact I was ill, and knew he had to 'hang in there' until I was better. I couldn't cope with social occasions, so he went by himself to birthday parties and dinners. He put one foot in front of the other, and just 'got on with things'.

My husband maintained the semblance of a normal life at home and he relied on our children to help him, both in practical and emotional ways. They had to do most of the shopping, the cooking, the washing and the cleaning. The load (especially for one of my daughters) was heavy. My husband talked to them about what was happening to me and about how he was feeling. It was very upsetting for them to have to support both their father and me. I had no idea.

There are some things I will never forget, and some I will never remember. There are times I cannot relive and things I cannot go back and change. There are people that I hurt.

Still, I am sure I am not on my own. We all do things we are not proud of. There are uncomfortable places everyone revisits from time to time.

The face of depression - Acrylic and pencil on paper 300 x 400mm

Beyond the breakers

Have you ever wondered how you might die? Have you stood on the platform of a train station and had a vivid image in your mind of what could happen if you stepped over the yellow safety line? Have you ever been waiting to cross the road and had shivers go up your spine thinking about accidentally tripping and falling in front of a car?

Have you stood on the balcony of a very tall building, and envisioned yourself leaning over the railing and falling in slow motion? Have you felt the rush of air and seen the ground fly up to meet you? Have you backed away, fearful you might impulsively do it, unable to stop yourself?

Have you ever gone swimming and been swept beyond the breakers?

I ran swiftly across the burning sand, splashing through the shallows on the deserted beach. I plunged into the water, bracing myself against the shock of the cold and began to swim strongly away from the beach.

It was dangerous and stupid to swim in the ocean when there was no one else around, but nothing had ever happened to me before. Besides, the water was glorious.

I swam hard, as I loved to do. It was exhilarating. I stopped and trod water for a while, then turned and looked back at the beach, which was now about two hundred metres away. I decided I should go back and started swimming towards the shore.

After a while I lifted my head. It was strange. The beach seemed further away, not closer. I put my head down again and stroked and kicked harder. Then I raised my head once more and looked towards the beach. It was even more distant.

In a heartbeat I knew what would happen. I would be pulled out further and further until the waves washed me around the headland into the open sea. I swam wildly now, splashing in panic, gasping and spluttering as I swallowed water.

'Stop it,' a voice sounded in my head. 'Don't be stupid. You know what you should do. Relax and swim across the rip, not against it.'

I forced myself to slow down my rhythm, to calm my breathing. I swam steadily, sideways, not straight towards the beach. I concentrated on my strokes. Left-right-left, breathe, kick-kick-kick. Right-left-right, breathe kick-kick-kick.

My shoulders ached. My rhythm was ragged and I kept swallowing water. I couldn't go on. I would never get there.

'Just twenty more strokes,' the voice in my head insisted. 'Just ten more strokes. Just five …'

I couldn't. Could I? I swam and swam and swam. Suddenly, something brushed my foot. A shark? Seaweed? Sand?

All at once I felt …

Panic
Fear
Terror
Dread
Horror
Desperation
Stupidity
Regret
Acceptance
Optimism

Relief

I knew one thing for sure. The next time I went to the beach (if there was a next time) I was going to swim between the flags.

Beyond the breakers - Oil on board 280 x 350 mm

In a mental hospital

A mental hospital is a place of sadness, sorrow, worry, criticism, anger, confusion, depression, discomfort, agitation, irritation, concern, fear and terror. A place where attention and concentration come and go, but never stay long enough to be of any use, where memory is annoyingly elusive. A place where thought processes and movements seem to be enveloped in a thick fog. A place where those on the outside wanting to help are tentative, unsure, fearful, anxious and desperately hopeful.

In such a place you can't concentrate enough to read or watch TV. You can't sleep because that's all you've been doing day and night and you're all slept out. You can't sit up, stand still or walk around, but what else is there to do?

Everything is sore. Your insides and your outsides, your hips, your shoulders and your neck. You have a headache you can't shift and you can't focus properly. You can't read or watch TV, because you can't concentrate enough.

Unwelcome thoughts surface and consume your mind. They circle, like vultures hovering over prey. On a good day they linger in the background. On a bad day they torment you unrelentingly. It's torture. Everyone in the ward is deemed to be 'acute'. Most are slow in movements, slow in speech, hunched in posture and downcast in mood. There are glazed eyes, dazed expressions and an occasional angry outburst.

Talk is of treatments, medication, ECT, memory loss, mood and how bad it is to feel like this and be in here, even though it's safe and you don't want to be anywhere else. The nurses dispense medication but not much else. The food is bland, but there's no point in complaining.

The group sessions are torture and if you are feeling anxious and agitated, or extremely sedated, it's hard to participate. It's impossible to sit still and concentrate for a whole session. It's really horrible being with so many depressed people.

The feng shui, atmosphere, vibe or whatever you want to call it is intensively negative. In the middle of summer, the air conditioner either doesn't work, or the temperature is set too high. Either way it is hot and stifling. You can't open the windows so there is no fresh air and if you're suicidal, they won't let you go outside. If you weren't already mad, you would go crazy after being in here for a day or so.

Most people stay in their beds where they feel the least stressed and a little safer. The biggest problem of all is the boredom. Time passes so slowly. The TV channels are limited to the off-ratings season, non-pay TV and the picture is white and snowy. The staff members don't seem to care. They're busy, but still …

There is absolutely nothing to do. If you weren't suicidal already this environment would be enough to make you want to kill yourself. Seriously.

They say this is one of the best hospitals in the country. It certainly costs a fortune to stay here. So why is there no activity room? No art and craft area? No pool table? No garden? No swimming pool? Why is the place so desolate and unwelcoming?

Visitors in the lounge are communal property. Everyone talks to them, well, those who feel like talking do. It helps to pass the time.

You are given drugs, of course, and the doctors and nurses tell you when you can and cannot have them. The medication will help you feel better, so you are told, but taking it comes at a price. Sedation brings calmness, but also that horrific, zombie-like state.

You are conflicted about becoming addicted to the tranquilisers and your anxiety escalates, feeding your obsessions. Then there is the hunger and the massive weight gain from the anti-psychotics. Within a very short space of time you look like you are nine months pregnant.

Visitors come, but really, you don't want them, not here, not like this. You do want to see them, of course, they are all so loving and caring, but you don't have the strength or confidence to reassure them that everything will be okay, because it won't be okay. Deep down you know, for sure, that nothing will ever be okay again.

Your visitors bring you books, magazines, flowers and chocolates. They try to make conversation. In fact, they have to do all of the talking. It's not easy for either of you, because you don't want to talk, but you feel obligated to try and 'entertain' them. It's impossible and pointless. Everything is such an effort.

All you want to do is feel better. You can't wait to leave, not because you really do want leave the safety of the hospital and your new friends, the only people you feel normal with and who you can relate to, but because it will mean you are better. Being allowed to go home will mean you are better.

You know that's a lie.

You will never be better.

Mental illness is an awful thing. A hidden thing. A shameful thing. That's how many people see it anyway. A thing to lie about to your friends and to family … well, not your family. They already know all about it, and they can't go back to a time when they didn't.

But everyone else can be kept in the dark. And if your family has to tell people something, a 'nervous breakdown' covers most things. It's vague enough for people not to know anything other than some kind of 'mental problem', without them actually knowing any of the details at all. Certainly there should never, ever be any mention of anything unsavoury or embarrassing.

When I was younger, at home with small children, and I had been feeling low or overwhelmed with the job of trying to be superwoman, I had occasionally thought a small stint in a psychiatric hospital might be just lovely. A little respite from the dramas of my life. A time to gently put down all of the balls I juggled so I could have a break from the feeling that if I dropped one, the lot would go. I could stay in bed all day, read and sleep. Someone else would do the cooking and washing up, look after the children and keep the household running. I thought it would be bliss.

However, I didn't know that these are precious things that one should not take for granted. I didn't know that participating in the ordinary rituals of life is not possible when you are in the middle of a 'nervous breakdown'. You can't choose to 'snap out of it', even when all you want to feel is normal (whatever that is), and all you desperately want to be able to do is something mundane like the washing up.

A 'nervous breakdown'. What does it mean? It means a profound lack of choice. It means being stuck in a state, absolutely terrified that this is what your life will be like permanently. Feeling so bad that you wish you were dead. Not being able to stop the bad thoughts running around and around and around your head. Over and over.

Thoughts that they will lock you up in some kind of hospital like something out of *One Flew Over the Cuckoo's Nest* for the rest of your life. Hating having to take the drugs that make you feel like a zombie. Disagreeing with the doctor's diagnosis, and not being able to coherently state your case, or to remember what questions to ask. Feeling so anxious or angry or agitated that you can't stand being in your own skin for another second.

In my skin - Ink, crayon and oil pastel on paper 100 x 100 mm

Suicide

If you take forty paracetamol tablets all at once they won't kill you.

Well, that's not exactly true. They will quite possibly kill you, but it won't be quick or easy. They will kill you slowly and painfully because your liver will pack it in, unable to break down the toxins in your body. If you're lucky you will end up with liver damage. If you're not you will need a liver transplant and if you're really unlucky you will die.

If you are really, really lucky and you get to the hospital within four hours and the antidote works you'll be fine. Physically fine that is. Your mental state will be another thing all together.

The doctor at emergency will give you the worst-case scenario when you arrive at casualty. That way if the results are good it is a bonus and if not, then you'll be prepared. The doctor will say, '*It only takes ten tablets of paracetamol. You don't need forty. You only need ten. Ten or forty, the liver processes it all at the same rate.'* It is scary because you can buy paracetamol at the corner shop.

When someone you care about tries to kill themselves it's awful for you and it's awful for them too. You won't be happy (of course), and they won't be happy either, when they come to consciousness and realised they're not dead. But you will forgive them everything because your relief will be so overwhelming that they are still alive.

I have written a lot of stories about (other people's) suicide attempts and suicides that have affected me. They are my stories, my experiences, and they have affected me deeply, but they are other people's stories too and I cannot tell my side without revealing theirs.

I would really love to talk about it more, but I can't.

Sometimes the things you have to leave out of a book are the most compelling.

Compelling - Ink, crayon and oil pastel on paper 100 x 100 mm

Tender sensibilities

Some years ago, the daughter of a close friend of mine I knew committed suicide.

Before her funeral I had been to other funerals, of course, but only to those of people I didn't know very well, or family members who were very old.

As a child I was sheltered from the realities and rituals of death. Death was referred to only in hushed adult whispers, not for children's ears. Children and young people were sometimes allowed to attend church services, but were never permitted to go to a cemetery. That was considered much too upsetting and completely unsuitable for tender sensibilities.

Consequently, at the age of fifteen, death had never been part of my life. I had never seen a dead body and I had never been to a funeral. I had never even thought about it until my holiday to Bali with my mother.

We were at a cremation ceremony. I stood in the middle of the Balinese village and looked, with a sense of shock and disbelief, at the body of a dead woman laid out on a concrete pillar in the middle of the open-air courtyard. Small children ran around as other family members, young and old, sat and talked or busied themselves with preparations for the funeral.

My mother and I were the only non-Balinese people there, and no one spoke to us, but strangely, I didn't feel out of place nor have the sense that I shouldn't be there. Despite the language barrier, we were made welcome, and if anything, I felt included, privileged, honoured and welcomed into the death ritual of a culture so different to my own.

The dead woman appeared to be very old, although never having seen a dead body before it was difficult to accurately judge her age. The woman lay on her back on the raised slab. She appeared to be sleeping peacefully, but I knew she wasn't. Her lips had sunk into her mouth where her teeth should have been, and she was completely still.

Looking at her was strangely comforting. It wasn't scary or upsetting. I really wanted to go up close to the woman but I thought it might be inappropriate, so I stayed where I was. No one cried or looked distraught. There were no raised voices and the people were calm and serene.

After a while the old woman's body was lifted onto a platform covered with a white cloth. It had a thatched, pitched roof and was supported by four white columns on a platform constructed of bamboo lengths tied together. Two or three people sat up with the body. The whole structure was then raised and lifted onto the shoulders of men from the village.

A group of musicians lifted a huge round metal instrument tied to bamboo onto their shoulders and then men gathered up drums and other musical instruments. The Gamelin orchestra played the cremation prayers.

The group carrying the dead woman progressed out of the courtyard and down the street, followed by the musicians and the other mourners. The procession stopped at every crossroad and the men slowly turned the platform 360 degrees before setting off again. This was to confuse the evil spirits, so that they would not follow the old woman into the afterlife.

People sat outside their houses and watched as the procession passed by. Even though the distance was short, it took a long time to progress from the village to their final destination. I watched with interest and amazement. I had not known where they were going or what would happen.

The procession arrived at the beach and the platform was set down in the water. Beautiful tropical flowers were thrown into the water. There were prayers for the journey into the afterlife. The platform was set alight and pushed out into the ocean.

I had not thought about the old woman and the cremation ceremony again until I was in the church at the funeral of my friend's daughter. It was in an old sandstone church. The service was sombre and restrained and the rituals were very different from the cremation ceremony for the woman in Bali.

The old woman's cremation ceremony had been a vibrant celebration of life whereas my friend's daughter's funeral was more of a subdued commemoration of death. Of course the events were very different. There were cultural, generational and age differences of course, however the most notable difference was the fact that the old woman had died of natural causes, whereas my friend's daughter had taken her own life.

The word suicide was not mentioned in the church, at the graveside, or at the wake, even though it was in the forefront of everyone's minds. In the silence were echoes of unspoken sentiments. Disgrace and dishonour. Sorrow and shame.

And it was, such a shame.

She died from depression. People die from depression, and bipolar disorder and schizophrenia, just as they die from cancer or a heart attack. Every day, in Australia, approximately six people commit suicide, and one hundred and eighty more attempt it.

When looking at statistics, I came across a website, <u>www.responseability.org</u>. Response Ability is an initiative of the Australian Government Department of Health and Ageing. According to their figures, around 2,100 people commit suicide in Australia every year. Suicide accounts for more deaths than transport accidents, and is the largest cause of death in the age group fifteen to nineteen years. It also suggests that around 11.9% of men and 16.6% of women in Australia will have suicidal thoughts in their lifetime.

When a person commits suicide, the loss, pain and grief suffered by family, friends and the community is profound and ongoing. However, apart from the families and friends of people who have committed suicide, no one seems to know much about this problem, or the extent of it. It is a hidden crisis, one only hears about in vague and general terms. The silence surely adds to the shame and stigma for everyone concerned.

For society things are changing but for individuals there is still a conspiracy of silence about this terrible killer.

We should all be talking about it, hearing about it, doing more about it and taking away the shame and stigma of it.

Tender sensibilities indeed.

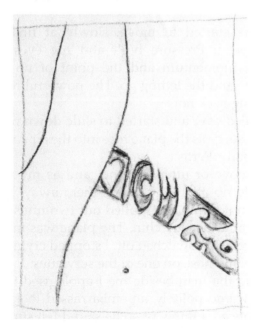

Beautiful - Charcoal on paper 300 x 400 mm

Moving forward

Confucius say: If you continue to live in the past your life is history

The diagnosis of mental illness came as quite a shock to me. I shouldn't have been surprised but I was. Stunned, shocked, shitty and sick. But as they say, life goes on.

I decided to take a trip, go away for a weekend by myself, to think it all through. To allow myself to grieve and wallow in shame and self-pity. I would hold it in until I had the privacy, space and time to deal with it all.

I boarded the plane, sat down, fastened my seat belt and organised my belongings. I examined my surroundings carefully, almost reverently. Turning my head to look out the window, I closed my eyes, anticipating what I knew was to come, what I had been suppressing since I had been given the news.

The plane started to move, slowly at first, then with increasing speed. Pressure built and my eyes welled up. Acceleration, momentum and the point of no return. The upward surge and the letting go. The powerful release. There was no turning back now.

Tears spilled over and started to slide down my face. I felt the powerful surge as the plane rose into the air and adrenaline flooded my body. Perfect.

I didn't move or utter a sound, and as my tears flowed freely, I made no attempt to wipe them away. Eventually, I reached down into my bag, pulled out two unused serviettes and held them under my chin. The plane was in the air now and the seatbelt sign switched off. I stopped crying, wiped my face and blew my nose on one of the serviettes.

Turning to the man beside me I apologised for making a fuss. He answered politely, an embarrassed look on his face. He hadn't noticed a thing, or so he said. I felt stupid then, for drawing it to his attention, even more compelled to offer some kind of explanation. He didn't seem the slightest bit curious, but I mumbled something about death and dying anyway.

It wasn't a lie. I felt as though I had died. What had happened to me could not be changed or undone. There was no point in trying to analyse or rationalise it. I had to just get through it and live with it the best way I could. I took a deep breath and turned to look out the window again.

The clouds cushioned the plane as the ground below me shifted in slow motion as the plane moved inexorably forward.

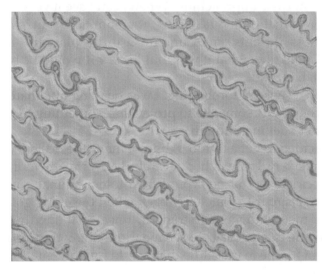

Inland rivers - Acrylic on canvas 410 x 510 mm

The cherry blossom tattoo

The idea came out of no-where, caught me off guard, and then crawled under my skin. I always thought they were common and in poor taste, labels proclaiming yourself to be not very nice or not very bright. I couldn't understand why anyone would want one.

Now I know why.

It's to be yourself, invent yourself, re-invent yourself and set yourself apart. To commemorate something that has happened to you. To pay homage. It's to live life on the edge, to push yourself, to prove something or to shock. Because life is too short. Because you have died and you are trying to shock yourself back to life. Or simply because you can.

People have had tattoos since ancient times, and the reasons and meanings behind tattoos are as numerous as the people who get them. In some cultures there is a deep and sacred connection between the skin and the spirit and they have therapeutic and healing qualities. Tattoos are an affirmation that your body is yours to have and enjoy while you are alive.

Tattoo #1 Strength

I was scared. I knew it was coming, the apocalypse, like I know when a storm is approaching. When I can't see it yet or hear it, but there's that ominous feeling, that familiar scent. The dogs get restless, the ants scurry and my arthritis plays up.

I didn't know what it was, but I knew it would be bad.

Bad, bad, bad.

I had a sense of foreboding. I was heading up. I had to find somewhere safe, someone to protect me, something to give me strength to get me through.

I decided to get a tattoo. I did not make the decision lightly or impulsively. I researched it carefully over many months.

I decided my tattoo would be a totem animal, my totem animal. A jaguar to watch my back when the going got tough, to give me courage and strength, unearth hidden gifts and connect me to my spirit. To see me through my transformation and fight for me in the battle that would fundamentally change who I was.

Suddenly I saw things differently, questioned my past beliefs about the world and everything I had ever known. I marked my body to pay my respects, to acknowledge and celebrate the reality that in life you can't ever go back.

Now I was different on the outside to match who I was becoming within. Covered by clothes, no one could see, no one knew I wasn't the old me. I liked looking normal on the outside, the same as I always had. People always judge a book by its cover.

Virgin skin, they call it, your skin before you get your first tattoo. People think it's painful, and it is, but pain is such a fluid experience. It's a different kind of pain.

This time, this first time, there was little pain, only adrenaline and excitement. This time, this first time, it didn't hurt at all. This pain was so good that when it ended I wanted more. I had found a way to feel a physical sensation to equal the excitement being stirred up in my mind.

It was exquisite. I was high.

'Maybe just one more time', I said to myself, and to the tattoo artist who gave me my jaguar. She laughed knowingly.

Tattoo #2 Sadness

Once again I did not take the decision to get another tattoo lightly or make it impulsively. I planned it carefully and waited. I couldn't get an appointment with the tattoo artist for eight months anyway. This time I wanted my tattoo to be a symbol that represented the story of my life. My old life and my new one. Black and grey, two halves of something, of someone who has been split asunder.

She snapped on her black latex gloves. As she shaved my skin and the cold shock of the disinfectant made me flinch. I stared at a framed photo of Jesus on the wall. Why would there be a religious photo in a tattoo parlour? And why could I hear country music in the background?

The tattoo machine started buzzing and the needles began piercing my skin, pushing into the bony, lowest part of my spine. I inhaled sharply, unable to breathe out again. As I held my breath I thought, 'I can't go through with this' but it was too late. I was there, leaning over a stool in a tattoo parlour and it had begun.

Terrible pain and agony were central to this experience. The needle plunged in over and over, up the center of my spine from the bottom of my tailbone to my shoulder blades and across to my rib cage. She paused only to wipe away the excess ink and blood as it pooled on my skin.

The pain was intense, sharp and excruciating. It was shocking.

Satisfying as only self-flagellation can be.

I had found a way to feel a physical pain to match my mental anguish, to distract my mind from the inner torment of severe depression.

The physical pain was so intense by the end it took all my strength not to vomit. I bit into my hand as the pain tore into me. Five and a half hours and it was still not finished.

'It's unbearable,' I whispered to the tattoo artist.

'Do you want me to stop?' she asked.

'No, I would never come back to finish it.' I answered.

She smiled. 'You'll be back.'

No I wouldn't. I was determined this would be the last one, the last time.

She laughed knowingly.

Tattoo #3 Splendour

I was happy and stable. Better. So much better.

In some cultures the cherry blossom heralds the return of spring, life and hope, the promise of summer after the long, dark winter. The natural beauty and grace not only refers to the flower, but to life itself. It captures the senses. There are more than five senses you know. There is sight, hearing, touch, smell and taste, of course, but also time, balance, pain, self, security, place and community. These senses are all damaged, compromised or destroyed because of bipolar, but revived by living well with it.

Cherry blossom flowers have dignity and strength. They are ephemeral and fleeting, as is life. The time we have on earth is short and fragile. We have to enjoy beauty wherever and whenever we can find it. I have that beauty with me now within in me and etched onto my body

My three tattoos, strength, sadness and splendor will be part of me always.

Spring - Pencil and charcoal on paper 190 x 270 mm

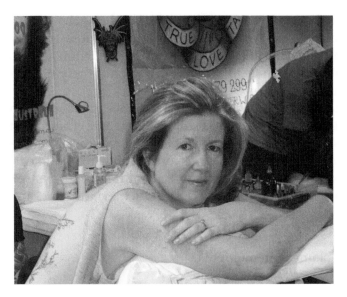

Life is short: get the tattoo

Don't blame it all on bipolar

There is an inherent conundrum about bipolar disorder, in fact about any mental illness.

What part of a person's behaviour is because of their own choice and what part is because they have a mental illness?

Here is my take on it. Let's assume you have been diagnosed with bipolar disorder. If your behaviour is 'normal' for you then it's you, but if your behaviour is really out of character for you (or simply not normal), then it is probably due to bipolar. Ridiculously vague, I know, but until there are definitive medical tests available (like brain scans or blood tests) to show one way or the other, that's all there is to go by.

If you have bipolar disorder you sometimes behave in uncharacteristic or antisocial ways because of it. That's a given. However, you can't blame everything on bipolar disorder. Not everything in your life happens because you have a mental illness. In particular, you can't blame all of your bad behaviour on bipolar. That's just a cop out.

You may have a mental illness, and it may cause you to behave badly when you are ill, but you also have your own personality and you have free will. You have choices and you can make your own decisions. You can choose to seek help. Or not. You can choose to take your prescribed medication. Or not. You might have bipolar disorder, and it might derail you at times, but you also have free will.

Many people with bipolar disorder do seek help and take their prescribed medication religiously. They don't take drugs or drink alcohol. When their behaviour starts to become different to how it normally is, or how they would like it to be, if they don't feel quite right, or if their family suggests it, they see their doctor and follow the advice they are given.

Take some responsibility.

Don't blame it all on bipolar.

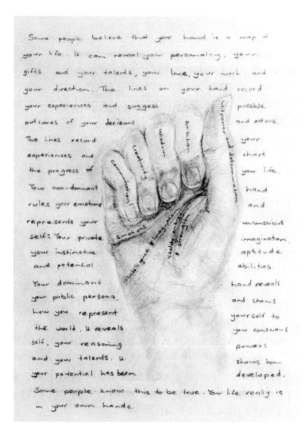

A map of your life - Pencil on paper 250 x 350 mm

Filling in forms

On your first visit to a doctor, dentist, chiropractor, massage therapist or any health professional, you have to fill in a questionnaire, giving your personal details and information about your health, including a list of the medications you normally take.

Fair enough. Health professionals need to have this information in order to treat you. Before my diagnosis of bipolar, I never gave it much thought. Now, however, it fills me with apprehension.

I always write down my illness and the names of my medications truthfully: Lamictal, Lithium and Seroquel. Sitting across from a doctor who is scrutinizing the form making comments, and asking questions, I stumble over the statement referring to my mental illness. So far so good. But then there are the inevitable questions:

'So what type of drug is Lamictal? I haven't heard of it.

What type of drug is Seroquel? I don't know that one either?'

They don't usually ask about Lithium. Most people know what Lithium is.

The answer to the first question is not too difficult,

'It's a mood stabilizer.'

This is generally understood and there is a relatively straightforward answer. However, the answer to the second is more difficult and always elicits a look of embarrassment, firstly from the health professional initially, and subsequently from me, as I say,

'It is an anti-psychotic.'

If you take an anti-psychotic the inherent implication is that you suffer from psychosis. I have never been psychotic, I take it primarily to help me sleep (my inability to sleep being a side effect of the Lamictal). I could say it is prescribed for me for sleep or hypomania or anxiety, but saying that doesn't sound much better, so usually I say nothing.

I'd love to say I have a rare and fascinating neurological disorder, and the medications I take have no description or classification. Or lie by omission and leave that part of the form blank. I am probably hypersensitive about it but I've had enough uncomfortable responses to be embarrassed a lot of the time.

73

Only one time did I have a different experience. I had to have a consultation with a plastic surgeon. Not for a facelift or liposuction, but for the removal of two very small moles. It was an ordinary appointment. I went into the waiting room and filled in the form, cringing slightly in anticipation of explaining to the specialist about my mental illness and my medications. I waited for a while, and was eventually called into his room. We sat across the table from one another and he went through the form.

He didn't mention the bipolar, but he did ask, 'What type of drug is Lamictal?' and I answered, 'A mood stabilizer'. I waited and he asked, 'What type of drug is Seroquel?' and I answered, 'It is an anti-psychotic.' He nodded his head.

He asked me to get up on the table, so he could examine the mole on my back and that is when he saw my tattoos. 'Wow' he said, 'They're lovely.' I was surprised, as most of the time no one says anything about my tattoos when they see them.

He finished looking at my back and returned to his desk. I sat back down opposite him once again.

'Do you mind me asking about your tattoos?' he said.

'No,' I answered.

He asked me when I got them, and why. I told him about my bipolar diagnosis and the reasons for each of my tattoos. He listened with what appeared to be genuine interest. The conversation was relatively brief, and then he got down to the business of removing my moles. Then the consultation was over and I went to the front desk to pay my bill.

I left his office feeling happy. Most health professionals made me feel uncomfortable about the whole bipolar thing. After three years, this specialist was the first one who had not been awkward and acted totally normally when talking to me about my mental illness.

It was so nice. I looked forward to the day it would happen again.

Resignation

When I was first diagnosed with bipolar disorder, my illness, together with the side effects of my medication, created difficulties for me in my workplace. I wasn't coping very well, so I took an extended period of leave and then I resigned.

Before I stopped work I had been teaching, lecturing and interpreting. My knowledge, skills and experience had been highly valued. I had been very happy with my job and proud of my achievements. I had been confident, passionate and enthusiastic and I felt incredibly lucky to have found such a rewarding career.

When I relinquished my job I gave up a lot. I missed having structure to my days and weeks. I missed my colleagues and my students. I missed using my brain and solving problems. I missed feeling useful and worthwhile. I felt guilty about not working and not contributing financially to my family.

Work is tied up so much with our identity and how we define ourselves. I am sure I am not on my own. Parents at home with young children and retirees may find it difficult to be out of the work force for some of the same reasons,

In social situations, a common conversation starter is the question, 'Do you work?'

If I said something like, 'I lecture medical students at Sydney University' (which I still do, albeit only once a year) people were usually very impressed.

If I said, 'I stay at home and look after my family,' they were usually not that impressed.

If I said, 'I don't work at the moment because I've got bipolar disorder' they were almost always embarrassed and ill at ease, even if I wasn't. When I did talk about my mental illness in casual conversation, I always wished I hadn't.

Disclosing a mood disorder in social situations is difficult, but it is even more difficult revealing it in the workplace. When I left work I did not want to 'burn my bridges' by disclosing my mental illness, and then regretting it. I had to weigh up my desire for understanding and acceptance with my fear of misunderstanding, prejudice and discrimination. Initially, I did tell a few close colleagues in confidence, ones I considered friends, to 'test the waters'.

While they tried to be supportive, their responses were mixed. One person refused to believe me and in a bizarre conversation I had to try and convince her that I really was mentally ill. Another seemed embarrassed, and suggested that perhaps this was 'personal information' and I should keep private. The third was initially supportive, but she soon became distant, and from then on, our relationship was uncomfortable and strained. I felt ashamed and embarrassed. The responses, from these people, who I thought would understand, did not inspire me to disclose my situation to anyone else at work.

I listened more closely to teachers talking in the staff room, and tuned into the gossip and lighthearted banter. I heard disparaging comments about mental illness from colleagues, well-educated and intelligent people, who would have been appalled to think they were being judgemental or prejudicial. Criticism and discrimination were inherent in every-day conversations, and the stigmatisation of those who were arbitrarily given a label of mental illness was usually nebulous and intangible.

My boss was a very professional, kind and compassionate man. I am sure he would have allowed me to talk about my illness without judgement or prejudice. I believe he would have treated my disclosure with sensitivity and confidentiality. I'd like to think he would have had some understanding of mental illness and its implications in the workplace. He certainly recognised and respected my personal strengths and capabilities. But something held me back. I felt ashamed, embarrassed and fearful. My conversations with my colleagues had made me wary. I was keenly aware that I couldn't take it back once I told him.

In theory, I knew that my rights should be protected by legislation, however, in reality I wasn't sure they actually would be. I was most concerned about confidentiality and privacy. I decided that disclosure would damage my professional reputation and compromise a return to work in the future.

I feared my boss may judge my disclosure, view my difficulties as incompetence and make assumptions about my behaviour based on the knowledge of my mood disorder. I worried he would treat me differently, and I knew he would be legally obliged to document my situation and inform others in the organisation. I was struggling to get well, to accept my diagnosis and come to terms with what was happening to me. It was not an easy time. When I left, I was very vague, and I spoke about 'health problems' being the reason for my leaving work.

Paradoxically, unemployment brought with it unexpected opportunities. I set new goals, expectations and ambitions (which were mainly to get well). I had the freedom and the time to do the things I wanted to, unencumbered by the restrictions of work. I was in a unique and privileged situation.

Many people I knew, especially the three work colleagues I had confided in, were envious. They would have loved to have given up work, stayed at home, looked after their families and had more time to themselves.

I like predictability, security and order. Change is difficult because it creates uncertainty. However, in work as in life, things are always changing. I have two choices. I can resist and resent it, or I can embrace its possibilities.

One of my favourite stories is a Chinese parable, *The Story of the Taoist Farmer*:

'A Chinese farmer has a stallion. One day the stallion runs away. The village people come to him and say, "Ah, such bad luck!" The farmer shrugs, "Good luck, bad luck, who knows?" A few days later the stallion returns with three mares. The village people come to him and say, "Ah, such good luck!" The farmer shrugs, "Good luck, bad luck, who knows?" The next week the farmer's son breaks his leg taming the wild mares. The village people come to him and say, "Ah, such bad luck!" The farmer shrugs, "Good luck, bad luck, who knows?" A month later the Chinese army comes and demands all the young men of soldier age. The farmer's son does not have to go because of his leg. The village people come to him and say, "Ah, such good luck!" The farmer shrugs, "Good luck, bad luck, who knows?" And so it goes...'

(Author Unknown)

You never know whether something that has happened to you is good luck or bad luck. Everyone has bad luck from time to time. What you see as bad luck can turn out to be good luck in the long run. You can take the opportunity to re-evaluate your life and find new and better directions.

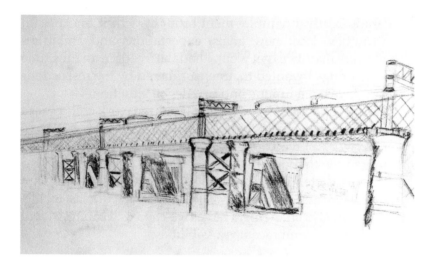

Meadowbank Bridge - Charcoal on paper 400 x 500 mm

Retirement

Now that I wasn't in paid employment any more, I could not say, 'I am a … and I work at …'

I was still the same person I had always been, but I could no longer define myself by what I did in the workplace. When you work, nobody questions how you spend your time. After my 'retirement' however, people often asked me, 'What do you do all day?'

I found it hard to answer them. I was busy, but doing things that no one would find interesting or of value. I was putting one foot in front of the other, trying to function so that my family could function. I was doing the shopping, cooking a basic meal every day and washing and ironing for a household of four people.

There is a huge loss of self that happens when you find you cannot work. The diagnosis of a mental illness does not change who you are, but it does change some things about you. I went from someone extremely capable in the workplace to someone 'disabled' and unable to work. I was now disabled by definition as well as dis–abled in practice.

Because of bipolar I was unable to do some of the things most other people could, things they took for granted, like going to work.

Once a person with a mental illness has had a major 'episode' and then recovered from it, it can take a long time for their level of cognitive processing to get back to normal functioning and each episode makes things worse.

My illness had affected my concentration, attention and ability to process information. How could I be capable and confident in the workplace if I had problems associated with cognitive deficit, even if it was only short term?

How could I be a competent employee if I could not show up for work on time, or cope with the demands of a complex and stressful or even simple and uncomplicated job? For years after I gave up work these issues remained raw and unresolved. Outwardly I was fine about it, but inside I wondered if I would always have a sense of loss about my inability to work in my previous career.

Some people choose not to work and love it. It's a lifestyle choice that's envied by many, those who work too hard and would love to stay at home. Not working as a consequence of a mental illness is not quite the same thing as not working because you decide not to.

Enforced leisure is not a holiday.

On the other hand, because I didn't work anymore I made the most of being at home. I was very happy to be able to pursue some of the things I couldn't when I was working. It was ironic. I was unhappy about not being able to work, but at the same time I loved the opportunity my mental illness gave me to stay at home.

I started doing things such as going to the library, reading (when I could concentrate), writing and catching up with friends. I woke up every morning and thanked God I didn't have to go to work that day, or the next. I savoured the pleasures inherent in taking life more slowly, and ignored the guilt about not being able to do too much. My husband was very supportive.

Sometimes I missed the structure of going to work. Little things, stupid things, like driving into the car park wondering if I would get the last car space and the pleasure it gave me when I did. I missed the cheerful banter in the staff room and reading with my students. I missed being able to make a financial contribution to my family and I missed the feeling of making a positive contribution to society.

I didn't miss all of it though. I didn't miss the stress, the planning, the preparation, the reports and the office politics. I knew I was still the competent teacher somewhere inside. I just couldn't do the job at that time, because of my mental illness. I could choose to be miserable about it and feel sorry for myself, which I did for a while. Poor me and all that.

But in the end I made a different choice. I chose not to cling to the belief that my fate had been decided by something other than myself, that my life was pre-determined, because of bipolar. I chose to believe that there were other things, wonderful experiences waiting for me in the future.

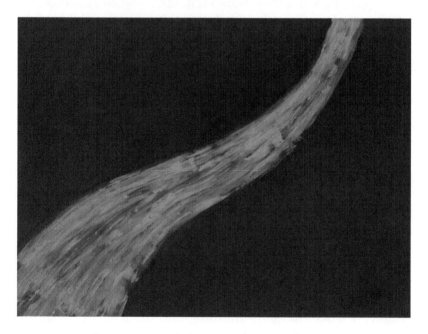

The road - Acrylic on canvas 700 x 1000 mm

Equilibrium

Recovery

'The distance between insanity and genius is measured only by success.' Bruce Feirstein

Recovery from bipolar disorder for me does not mean cure, it means management. It is not something I can resolve once and for all, and then put it behind me, rather it is an ongoing process. I am vigilant, even when I am well. Especially when I am well.

For me, recovery from my mental illness means being stable (mostly), living without symptoms (mostly) and being able to function well.

To get to this place I had to get the correct diagnosis in the first place and then accept that I did (do), indeed, have a mental illness. I had to find a psychiatrist, see him (now her) regularly (every week for the first two years and now every few months), follow his (her) advice and take the (constantly changing) medication.

I needed to find out as much as I could about my illness, so I read books and accessed a wealth of information, through organisations such as The Black Dog Institute and SANE. I attended wellness programs and went to talks, lectures and seminars.

I went to a support group where I talked to and learned from others in a similar situation. I learned how to channel my mental illness into positive pursuits such as writing, drawing and painting. I nurtured supportive close relationships with my family and friends.

I am still finding out about myself and how my illness presents and affects me. I am still learning to recognise my triggers and early warning signs, both avoidable and unavoidable ones. And even though I take my medication religiously, I still swing. Not wildly, but more than I would like to.

One of the most important aspects of my recovery is not being too hard on myself.

Happiness

'Blessed are the cracked, for they shall let in the light.' Groucho Marx

Mental illness has taught me to question some common assumptions.

Happiness is the most important thing in life.

The quest for happiness seems to be all-important in our society and something to strive for. There are books and conferences devoted to the subject. But is happiness the 'be-all and end-all'? Do you have to be happy for life to be good? I'm not always happy and my life is great. Besides, I think there are more important things in life than happiness. Kindness for one.

Your past will always define you.

You can't change your past but you can change the stories you tell about your past, and when you change your stories you change your understanding of your past. Simple.

Success is good and failure is bad.

Failure is not the opposite of success. Failure is the opposite of never having tried. Of never taking risks. Failure is the basis of success, a necessary ingredient.

What people think of you is really important.

What people think of you is important if you let it be. The opinions of the people who understand and care do matter, and the opinions of the people who don't, don't.

Loss is always terrible.

Loss might always be hard, and sometimes there is no redemption in a tragic situation, but sometimes good things can come from loss.

Persistence, perspicacity and providence

Persistence: Doing something steadily over time, despite problems or difficulties
Perspicacity: The ability to judge quickly what is happening in a situation
Providence: Fate, chance or luck

One of my heroes is a man named Stephen Bradbury, an ice-skater from Queensland. Through a combination of persistence, perspicacity and providence, he became the first Australian to win a gold medal in the Winter Olympics. For those who don't know the story, Stephen Bradbury was competing in the short track speed skating final in the 2002 Winter Olympics, racing against an American skater, a Chinese skater, a Korean skater and a Canadian skater.

Bradbury had trained hard for twelve years, and he had faced many setbacks and challenges during that time. He had sustained some horrific injuries in training, including breaking his neck in a fall on the ice and nearly dying of blood loss after having his leg cut open by a skate.

In reality, it was always going to be difficult (if not impossible) for him to become the world champion. In an interview after the race, Bradbury said he had just wanted to skate his best.

Bradbury was at the back of the pack, hoping against hope to win a bronze medal, although that seemed highly unlikely. Heading into the final turn, the Chinese skater fell. Then, incredibly, the other three skaters got caught up and they fell over too. Bradbury was far enough behind to navigate his way around the pile of skaters without falling over. All he had to do was concentrate, be careful and stay upright until the finishing line, which he did.

Stephen Bradbury won the gold medal, against all the odds. Some people said he won it by accident. Bradbury said that he accepted the gold medal, not for the thirty seconds of the race, but for the twelve years leading up to it.

It's kind of like that with mental illness. There are three things you need. Persistence, perspicacity and providence. You have to make plans and prepare, work steadily over time (despite the inevitable problems and difficulties) and keep an eye on what is going on. Then, when an opportunity comes your way (and it will), you just have to be careful, concentrate and put one foot in front of the other. When persistence, perspicacity and providence align, wonderful things can happen.

Just ask Stephen Bradbury.

A passion for painting

I wrote this chapter when I was very ill and intertwined my feelings and words with the words of authors including James Elkins, David Bayles and Ted Orland. This chapter is a synthesis of their words and mine.

Because of bipolar, I learned how to paint.

Before bipolar, I had no interest, experience, talent or training in arts, but when I was (unknowingly) becoming manic, I decided I would learn to paint. It was a very random thing, and the idea came upon me suddenly, out of no-where. I knew in my mind exactly what I wanted to do, and that was to paint large works and hang them all through my house.

I looked up the profiles of various Sydney artists and chose one whose work I adored. I e-mailed him and asked if he gave individual art lessons. I am sure he thought it was a bit strange to be approached out of the blue, by someone he didn't know, but he took me on and mentored me. I don't think he realised how little I knew about painting (which was nothing at all) or how much I valued (and still value) his mentorship.

I had half a dozen lessons with him and he taught me so much, not only about art, but also about life. When my private lessons with him finished, I stumbled across a free TAFE course for people with a mental illness. I enrolled and studied there one afternoon each week for eighteen months.

There was a wonderful freedom in studying art in this class. I had nothing to lose and nothing to prove. No one expected anything from me so I was free to do anything, or nothing at all. If I couldn't manage to stay for the full three hours, I went home early. If I couldn't manage to get there at all, that was fine too.

When the course finished, I felt much better. I was ready to take on something more challenging and, with the encouragement of my TAFE teacher, I decided to go to art school. I sat a drawing test, presented a portfolio, had an interview and and was surprised and delighted to be accepted as a first year student. I still wasn't well, but it was a step in the right direction.

I studied painting and drawing (two subjects at a time) at art school for two years and during that time my mental health improved enormously. I was on better medication and becoming much more stable.

For a while painting became my passion, focus, commitment and struggle. When I was painting time stood still. When I finished a painting, for a brief moment I could look at my creation and it would speak to me softly, radiating energy, intensity, integrity and purity.

intangible
intense
insistent
indescribable

intoxicating

The rhythmic motions of the brush were soothing. It was pleasurable, frustrating, intuitive, hypnotic, alluring and addictive. Most definitely addictive.

Experimentation was the key, trying to make disparate connections and link unrelated things to see something new, say something new. It was about the magical moment when a painting (drawing, sculpture or installation) suddenly stopped looking flat and came alive, taking on a vibrancy, a life and a personality all of its own. I would experience the fleeting sense of freedom that comes with unadulterated pleasure.

Inevitably though, I would come back down to earth. My rational mind would take over and I would be dissatisfied with my work. I would no longer be so sure of myself, or my art or my recovery.

Self-criticism is not exclusive to those with a mental illnesses, it is inherent in the human experience. Who doesn't desire approval, acceptance, understanding and the critical acclaim of others? In any creative endeavor, doubt and negative self-talk always come into play. But, as Andre Gide, French novelist and essayist wrote,

'One does not discover new lands without consenting to lose sight of the shore for a very long time.'

So I set sail, consenting to lose sight of the shore for a long time. I knew that to discover new lands I had to leave the old ones behind, the safe, comfortable, familiar places I knew so well. I had no map to take with me and I knew there was risk and danger but I searched for true north, set a course and moved forward with faith, courage and persistence.

Not even when I was lost and far from home did I give up. Not even when I was drowning.

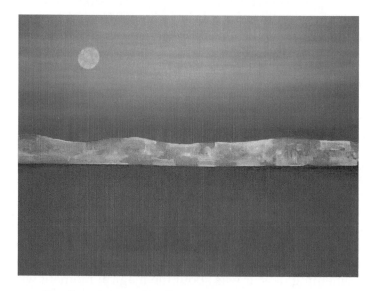

Far from home - Acrylic on canvas 700 x 1000 mm

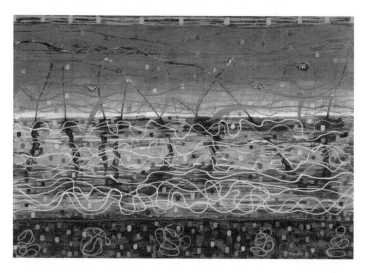

Landscape of the mind - Acrylic on canvas 700 x 1000 mm

Landscape of the mind

Orange is a nice place to be
but yellow can be nicer still

It is tempting to reach up
higher into the pale blue

Surge upwards
fly higher and higher
until there is no more sky

Red is the upper limit
unyielding and unforgiving
the catalyst
for an inevitable implosion

Fiery shards spew over the land below
raining down into the abyss

Red filaments twist
and turn in on themselves
paying the price
for having flown so close to the sun

The traces and marks
layers and lines
embody the texture

complexity and substance
of the inner landscape
of the mind

Be daring, be different

From art school and my mentor, I learned that:

- Creative pursuits have their own seasons. There are times when things flow in an uninhibited way and there are times when nothing happens.
- There is a very fine line between a masterpiece and a big miss.

- Disasters will happen and that is desirable. You learn the most from making mistakes.
- You have to find your own way. No-one else can do it for you.
- Twenty people can paint the same thing and you will have twenty different paintings.
- Painting and drawing make you more aware of your visual world and enable you see things differently and to see things you would not have otherwise seen.
- Creating art goes far beyond the mere ability to record images on paper, just as writing goes far beyond the ability to put words on paper.
- The whole point of creating a piece of art, rather than just talking or writing about it, is that it embodies things that cannot be put into words.
- You will only succeed if you are enthusiastic, open-minded and curious.
- What's important is to keep learning, growing, evolving and most of all enjoying yourself in the process.
- The techniques of making art are important but the creative process has greater significance.
- Making art is a present time and personal experience. It cannot be anything else.
- Creating art takes time, but you can manipulate time. You can make it fly and at the same time make it stand still.
- You can reach a sense of equilibrium through art and it can support you through a difficult time in your life.
- Creating art can give you a sense of release, make you feel better about the world and more optimistic for the future.

When I was at art school, what drove me was the process as much as the finished product and the desire to express myself and communicate with others the only way I could. It left behind a residue of personal freedom, pleasure and a sense of accomplishment that I still feel today. A feeling that I cannot summon at will, but in having experienced it, I know it exists, and have hope that I can experience again in the future.

When I was at art school the most important thing I learned is that originality is easy to copy but not so easy to achieve. Being different is a blessing not a curse and (as an artist) it is much more important to be different from others than to be the same as everyone else. Being unique is a positive thing, something to aspire to and to be proud of, because artistic difference is an artist's biggest asset.

When I was at art school and people asked me what I did, I said I was an artist. As I see it, if you do something you call art and you say you're an artist, then you're an artist. If you believe it, then other people will too.

You're not alone

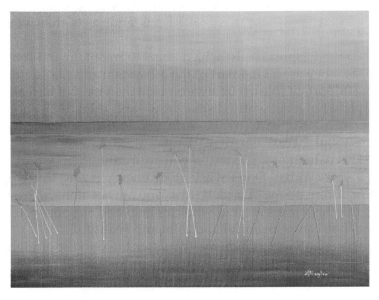

You're not alone - Acrylic on canvas 700 x 1000 mm

One of my paintings is of crows perched on poles in the water. The darkness is fading and the new day just beginning. The sunrise is a vista of oranges, reds and yellows.

At first glance, you don't know they are crows as they have taken on the hue of the dawn.

There are many crows around, but perched on their individual poles, each one is alone. They are calm and serene and for the moment all is well with the world. The solitude suits them just fine. If they need to talk to another crow, they know they only have to look around, or call out.

I am like one of those crows. I have to go through the dark nights by myself, but there are other crows around me who can make me feel less alone, simply because they are crows too.

Most people don't like crows, and would never want to be one. They are a frightened by the noises they make, the way they look and by some of the things they do. They would much prefer to be with 'nicer' birds, like rainbow lorikeets.

Some crows appreciate the benefits of being a crow and are happy with it. Others would rather be lorikeets, but if they could become a lorikeet, they might find out that life for lorikeets is not all it's cracked up to be for them either.

Ornithologists say that crows are the most social and intelligent of all birds. They are creative about how they catch and store their food. They eat insects and pests that would otherwise damage crops.

They transport seeds, which helps to maintain and renew forests. They are a vital part of the ecosystem and play a much more important role in our environment than most of us realise. People who vehemently dislike crows and think they should be eradicated might change their minds if they understood more about them.

This painting says to me, 'if you are a crow, then be the best crow you can be'. Don't waste your energy trying to change into a different type of bird. It says, 'you are not alone, there are lots of other crows around who can help and support you'. It says, 'Life can be peaceful and calm and beautiful'.

This painting reminds me that after the darkest of nights, the sun will always rise, often to a beautiful dawn.

The elephant in the room

When I started at art school I was excited and optimistic. My life was changing and I was moving forward with confidence, passion and enthusiasm. I felt incredibly lucky to have found a new path, a new purpose.

My course gave structure to my life and something to get out of bed for. Two days a week I had to get up, get dressed, get out of the house and go to art school. If I hadn't, then what would I have done?

Walked the dog? Maybe. Tidied the house? Maybe not. Done the shopping? I hate shopping.

Cooked the meals? I hate cooking even more than shopping. Gone to the library? There are only so many books you can read.

It is lonely and isolating spending all day by yourself if you don't go to work and don't have anything else to do. I loved drawing and painting and I was so full of enthusiasm for art school at the beginning of the year, but after six months I wasn't so sure. It was winter, and my mood wasn't all that stable. My mental illness thing was becoming difficult to manage and it was impacting on my art studies. Not being well was one thing. Talking to my teachers about it was quite another.

It wasn't that they were unsympathetic or unsupportive, but most of them were a bit weird about it. Some of them were a lot weird about it. I didn't want to feel embarrassed and awkward but some of them clearly were, and their difficulties made me uncomfortable, when I wouldn't otherwise have.

One woman in particular, a gentle and sensitive teacher, could not acknowledge it or even make eye contact with me when I tried to talk to her about it. She was kind and compassionate I could tell, but she couldn't cope with talking about it. This was the gist of one of our conversations:

Me: 'I am a disability student and I have been allocated some extra support time.'

Her: 'You don't look disabled to me.'

Me: 'I have a mental illness.'

Her: 'Er...oh........ (Looks away and changes the subject).'

Whenever I tried to say something to explain how it impacted on my attendance or my work her eyes would glaze over and she would quickly change the topic of conversation. How could I make her listen to me and actually hear what I had to say? Why couldn't she answer my questions about reasonable accommodation and support? I decided that if I could not talk to her face to face, I would send her an email.

I thought she couldn't ignore that. This is part of what my e-mail said:

> 'Hi …. I have bipolar disorder, a condition I battle to keep under control. I have been unwell since the end of last term, which is why I have missed some classes and left others early. I am really sorry. It must seem rude for me to just leave without saying anything. I plan to come to class regularly but if I am not able to attend I hope you will understand. There may be times when I come, but find I cannot stay for the full three hours. I may also need to make some modifications to my end of year assessment. The TAFE psych disability support teacher can liaise with my teachers about assessment if necessary. Please feel free to talk to me openly about any of this. I am very happy to discuss it with you and answer any questions you may have. Kind regards …'

I waited for a reply. One or two words of acknowledgement from her would have been fine. 'Thanks' or 'That's okay' or 'See you on Monday.' But there was no reply that day, or the next, or the one after. I wondered if she had received my email. I waited until my next class to see her and to talk about it, but she wasn't there. She was away, sick. I would have to wait another week to see her. I was really stressing about it by now.

I decided to put a copy of my email in her pigeonhole in the staff room to make sure she had received it. There was no reply to that either so I had to wait until the next class. When I walked in, she was there, and she nodded her head at me. I raised my eyebrows and she said 'I got your e-mail.'

I asked why she hadn't replied, and she said she thought I wasn't on the internal e-mail. That made no sense. All she had to do was press reply.

And I did have an art school student e-mail address, but … fine, whatever.

At the next class I approached her to ask about the end of year assessment tasks. I wanted to know if I had sufficient works in my portfolio to satisfy the requirements for the end of year assessment, and if I did not, what I should do about it. I also wanted to check that my attendance record was OK.

I said, 'Hi … Can I talk to you about the end of year assessment?'

She leaned towards me, patted my forearm, and said with a sympathetic, (or perhaps condescending) smile, 'You'll be fine, don't worry you'll be fine.'

It would have been so much better if, instead of patting my arm, she had said something normal, the way she would to any other student.

I didn't want anything heavy. I just wanted for her to be able to listen to me say, 'I have a mental illness, but that's okay. I am the same as anyone else, I just have a few different needs, and this is what they are ....'

Was it too much to expect her to look me in the eye and say 'That's fine, no worries' or 'Sure, let me know what they are'? Obviously she couldn't.

It was unmentionable.

My mental illness, the elephant in the room.

What did I learn from this experience? I learned I had to have a thicker hide. I learned that not everyone will be comfortable with my mental illness and I learned that I have to be OK with that. I learned that sometimes I just have to live with discomfort, both other people's and my own.

Out of your mind - Acrylic on canvas 300 x 400 mm

Never say never

I was going to art school two days a week. On the other three days I was just enjoying being alive and looking after my family. I was starting to feel as though my life was finally under control. I was better, much better.

Then came the conversation with my husband about money, or to be precise, the lack of it. I needed to go back to work ASAP. The GFC and all that. After complaining about not being able to work, and then finding a life outside of it, I was going back.

From this I learned two things: be careful what you wish for and never say never.

Worse things happen at sea - Oil on canvas 610 x 760 mm

My exciting new life

So here I am with my exciting new life
trying not to get myself into strife
(but always, opportunities are rife)

My mood is neither too high or low
my life is not too fast or too slow
(challenges abound, but I always have a go)

Whenever I start to head up high
I won't let myself soar to the sky
(I miss it, but really, I just shouldn't fly)

I know I'd just come crashing down
and stay at home in my dressing gown
(with a heavy heart and permanent frown)

Disheartened and depressed I'd stay in bed
feeling like I was dead
(and crazy in the head)

I'd be sick and then fine
I don't want that this time
(but bipolar is never benign)

I don't look like I've got it
not even a little bit
(people say "You? Not in a pink fit")

However, a plan I have devised
and people would be really surprised
(if only they just realised)

Acceptance is crucial, you have to know
and it's vital to change the status quo
(read on, more is revealed below)

Anonymity is key for people like me
as others judge and will not see
(no-one with bipolar is ever free)

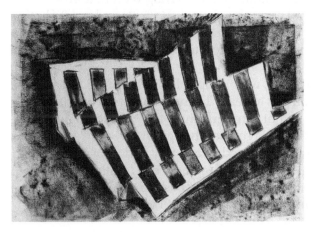

Black and white - Charcoal on paper 410 x 590 mm

The outing

I shouldn't have written this book
said a voice in my ear

Was it me who said it
or one I held dear?

It sprang from anger
protection and fear

and the message was clear

Shame on me for writing this book and wanting to publish it.
Shame on me for putting my name to it and for talking about it.
For exposing myself and in doing so, exposing others.

I shouldn't have.

I will lose my job. It will destroy my life and my husband's
too. We will be humiliated and worse. Our children as well.

My siblings will be 'outed' as having a sister with a mental
illness. I should have thought about that, about their shame.
How could I do this to them?

Don't I know that people can talk about having depression,
but not bipolar disorder? Do I not understand that people are
scared of people like me? It is the last frontier. No, it's not right,
but it is just the way the world is.

Do I really want to be the one to raise my head above the
parapet? Why not leave it to other people to blaze the trail?

Is it just the challenge? Is it to say I'm an 'author'. Why not
write fiction then? What's wrong with fiction?

Is it not enough to have just written a book? That's a success
in and of itself? Congratulations. It is a wonderful achievement
that someone wants to publish it. Why can't I be satisfied with
that?

Okay then, why not publish just a few copies for myself and
for my family to read. Then I can say it's officially published.

Do I not understand the consequences of general
publication? Have I not thought it through? Why have I not sat
down and examined every tiny little possibility of the things
that could happen to me and my family as a consequence of
public exposure? Perhaps bad things won't happen, but they
could, and then where would I be?

What about the stigma? The shame, disgrace and the dishonour than emanates from those around me, but also from within? Haven't I internalised the stereotypes I grew up with? People with bipolar disorder are sick, abnormal, different, odd, dangerous, unstable, unreliable, unpredictable and violent. Aren't they?

Just read the newspapers, listen to the radio or watch TV.

The media are not to be trusted, everyone knows that. They twist things and for some, their 'raison d'être' seems to be to ruin people's lives for the sake of a good story. Why on earth would I invite that scrutiny?

Why?

This is why.

To help people. People like me and people like you and people like 'them'. To stand tall and proud and say this is who I am and this is what has happened to me. To say I have done nothing wrong and I will not be shamed. To raise awareness, to inform and to educate.

To improve attitudes towards those of us who live with, and struggle with, and triumph over, bipolar disorder, depression or any type of mental illness. To challenge stereotypes and to fight stigma. To show that recovery is possible and to convey hope.

To speak for those who do not have a voice.

But it's easier said than done. Community perceptions and attitudes are changing for the better and that's great, but we still have a long, long way to go. Unfortunately, ignorance, stigma, stereotyping, discrimination and prejudice abound.

It's scary to have a mental illness and even more scary to tell people about it.

But if no one speaks out …
    … and no one comes out …
        … how do things change?

There's one in every family

The future

What is the future for people with bipolar disorder? In many ways, life for people living with mental illness now is much better than it has ever been in the past, but in other ways we are still in the dark ages.

The scientific literature tells us that much progress is being made, and it is and I believe that most strongly. There are continual and exciting advances in treatments, drugs and other therapies. Regarding stigma and discrimination I am not so sure that progress is happening at the same rate. As for the future, who knows?

Treatment

For me personally, in terms of treatment, I continue to seek out the medications I tolerate the best, and put up with the side effects. I persist with the ongoing challenge of getting the mix just right, the continual trade-offs between the benefits and the side effects. I do everything I can to prevent relapse. I anticipate my triggers and intervene early. I force myself to go to bed at a reasonable time, as I know that sleep is crucial. I exercise and eat a diet of vegetables, fruit, meat, fish and whole grains.

I don't eat all the nice things in life such as chocolate, biscuits, junk food, meat pies, processed meats, pizza, chips, hamburgers, white bread, sugar or soft drink. I take fish oil and vitamin supplements. I don't smoke or drink and manage stress to the best of my ability.

I do all of these things religiously except, of course, when I don't.

Like tonight. It is 1.00am and I have just polished off eight chocolate marshmallow biscuits, one after the other. When things fall apart and I am back on the chocolate biscuits and chips, and not exercising or sleeping properly, I eventually get my act together and I try again. And again.

That's what I do. That's all anyone can do.

Stigma and discrimination

Regarding stigma and discrimination, I take every opportunity to educate people who don't know anything about bipolar disorder or mental illness and I do my best to empower those who do.

I am lucky. I have a supportive, loving family, and a few very close friends who understand and don't care about my mental illness. I have a job that I love, and (hopefully) am good at.

I am courageous and strong and I am continually surprised by the hidden talents and strengths I find within myself.

I celebrate every day, because however long I live, my life will be over in a flash.

Celebrate every day - Charcoal on paper 200 x 300 mm

A good life

What constitutes a good life?

We all have things we want to achieve for ourselves and for our children. I was brought up to value things like tertiary education, social status, professional employment, wealth and home ownership.

Personal qualities such as intelligence, and being literate and articulate were, and still are, highly regarded in my family. They are also valued highly in our society. And I think it's good to want these things for ourselves and for our children.

I am lucky, very lucky to have been able to achieve some of these things. But what about people who do not or cannot achieve any of them? People whose mental illness precludes them. Or people like my son.

After my son was born with Down syndrome, I had to re-think my goals, expectations and ambitions for him, and really, for myself and my other children as well.

I have learned that it doesn't matter if people cannot achieve these things. Their lives can still have meaning and purpose, and be worthwhile and successful because there are other indicators of success in life.

Things like doing your best, overcoming adversity, having good self-esteem, achieving your potential whatever that might be, being a positive person, relating well to others, having a sense of humour, enjoying your work, making a difference in other people's lives, being part of a family, having good friends and getting up every morning looking forward to the day. Enjoying the life you have. My son achieves all of these things. Everyone can.

Raising my son has helped me to deal with my own mental illness. I have never been ashamed or embarrassed about his intellectual disability and so I should not be ashamed of my own mental illness. My son's life is so much more difficult than mine, and yet he is an inspiration to me. These are just some of the things I love about him:

He is always refreshingly honest, straightforward and unpretentious. As the saying goes, 'What you see is what you get'.

He loves a simple life, with order and structure.

His room is always tidy and his things are arranged 'just so'

He empties the bins and un-stacks the dishwasher without being asked.

He likes to know, in advance, what is on the menu for dinner every night of the week and he rings me every day to make sure I am organised.

He and his friends really know how to have a good time. Rather than standing around the edges at parties, looking embarrassed, they are all up on the dance floor as soon as the first song is played. Not being able to dance is no excuse for not dancing, therefore there is no need for anyone to feel foolish or be embarrassed.

He loves his work and is happy to have a job. He never wants to stay home, even when he is sick and he never complains. Having a job is a wonderful thing, a privilege.

In coming to terms with my mental illness, these are the things I have learned from my son about how to live a happy life, regardless of the challenges you face. These are the things he has taught me:

- Do the best with what you've got and don't compare yourself with others.

- Wear the clothes you like regardless of what other people think or say.

- Enjoy the simple things in life – food, music, family, friends.
- Exercise your right to choose – take advantage of your choices in life.
- Value your independence.
- Accept help when you need to.
- Say sorry when you know you have done the wrong thing.
- Understand that one or two really good friends are all you need.
- Know that being kind is so much more important than being clever.
- Hold on tightly to the things you really love.
- Give away the things you don't need.
- Don't hold grudges.
- Be yourself.
- Live in the moment and enjoy what you are doing right now.

So, what does constitute a good life? I think it is making the most of the one you've got.

My party clothes

I love collage.

I see images in magazines, or elsewhere, that resonate with me because of their subject matter, style, artistic or creative qualities. I collect them, cut them out, look at them, think about them and then plan and arrange them in a way, and a form, that pleases me.

I take disparate images, select, combine and arrange (and re-arrange) them so that when I am finished I am not conscious of the juxtaposition, but of the work as a whole. Everything absorbs, reflects and informs everything else.

For me, creating a collage is like a five year-old dressing to go to a party wearing all her favourite clothes. The sparkly glittery hot pink top with the miss-matched skirt and gum boots, the old fashioned handbag, and the fluffy jacket. The bling ring and the tiara. It can look terrible, but then again, as a whole outfit, it can look absolutely fabulous.

Mistake or masterpiece? It's not always in the eye of the beholder.

I am that five year-old, putting all of my favourite things in this book. My tastes are eclectic and I like it that way.

This book is a collage. Pieces of me, combined and arranged just so. I didn't write it all at once and there were sometimes years between chapters, but when I decided to assemble everything I had written, this book took shape. A collage of vignettes, eclectic and uniquely me. Just like my party clothes. If you like some of my stories, that's great, but if you don't that's fine too, we all have different tastes.

I may sometimes look a bit ridiculous, but that doesn't matter. These are my favourite party clothes and I love wearing them.

Pieces of me - Multimedia 450 x 600 m

If at first you don't succeed

If at first you don't succeed
then try, try again

If at first you don't succeed
and you've tried and tried again
then maybe you should try something else

If at first you don't succeed
and you've tried and tried again
then maybe you should just be happy with what you've got

If at first you don't succeed
and you've tried and tried again
and you've tried something else
then maybe you should give up

If at first you don't succeed
then don't take up anything too dangerous
(like hang gliding)

If at first you don't succeed
just think how many people you've made very happy,
like everyone who wants to get their own book published

If at first you don't succeed
Press delete, delete, delete

If at first you don't succeed
then re-define success
As for me …

If at first I don't succeed
I try and try again

If at first I don't succeed
and I've tried and tried again
then I weep and wail

If at first I don't succeed
and I've tried and tried again
and I've wept and wailed
then I rant and rave

and then

I carry on

Although I am very tempted
to press delete, delete, delete
I don't

I hang in there and wait
until a new challenge comes along

and I succeed

One perfect day

The secret to having it all is believing you already do

One hundred and one things to do before I die

When you have a serious illness, a chronic or life threatening one, as bipolar disorder can be, or when you go through a big bumpy patch in life, you question lots of things like:

Why are we here? What is life about? What do I want to achieve in my life?'

I don't want to get to the end of my life and regret not having done things, be they large or small, important or trivial, momentous or insignificant.

I want to celebrate life and I have written a list of the 100 things I want to do before I die.

Some, like winning Lotto or giving a million dollars to charity are extremely unlikely to happen, but others, like growing roses and seeing Rod Stewart in concert, are certainly achievable.

I have ticked the things I have already achieved. I am working on the rest.

Life is short, and I don't want to die wondering, so this is my bucket list:

1. Go snorkelling (√)
2. Have children (√)
3. Take a helicopter ride (√)
4. Watch the sun rise on a tropical island (√)
5. Collect donations for charity (√)
6. Learn sign language (√)
7. Get a master's degree (√)
8. Be a stay at home mum (√)
9. Be a working mum (√)
10. Have a long and happy marriage (√)
11. Get a tattoo (√)
12. Learn to paint (√)
13. Ride on an elephant (√)
14. Lecture at university (√)
15. Have an in-depth discussion with a Buddhist monk (√)

16. See Elton John and Billy Joel in concert (√)
17. Join a choir (√)
18. Visit the Great Barrier Reef (√)
19. Sing at the Opera House (√)
20. Learn CPR (√)
21. Drive an expensive sports car (√)
22. Teach a child to read (√)
23. Swim with a triathlon squad (√)
24. See my children grow up (√)
25. Hire a tropical island for a weekend for 10 of my closest friends (√)
26. Pay off the car (√)
27. Throw someone a surprise party (√)
28. Go on a cruise (√)
29. Work with a mentor (√)
30. Have an article published (√)
31. Experience other cultures (√)
32. Sell stuff on e-bay (√)
33. See Rod Stewart in concert (√)
34. Climb a mountain (√)
35. Learn ballet (√)
36. Visit central Australia (√)
37. Have a painting in an art exhibition (√)
38. Win a prize in a writing competition (√)
39. Have professional photos taken (√)
40. Make a record (√)
41. See original paintings by Monet and Van Gogh (√)
42. Work with children who have disabilities (√)
43. Save someone's life (√)
44. Sell a painting (√)
45. Write a blog (√)

46. Be a volunteer (√)
47. Find a fossil (√)
48. Publish a book (√)
49. Have piano lessons (√)
50. Work in a job I love (√)
51. Sign up to be an organ donor (√)
52. Go in writing competitions (√)
53. Create a vegetable garden
54. Meet Kay Redfield Jamison
55. Learn to take great photographs
56. Win the lottery
57. Play in a band
58. Grow roses and sweet peas
59. Meet the Dalai Lama
60. Buy beautiful flowers for the house every week
61. Donate blood
62. Learn how to love cooking
63. Live without TV for a year
64. See Raul Malo in concert
65. Have a feng shui consultation
66. Learn how to compost
67. Invest in the stock market
68. Buy an exquisite wardrobe of clothes and shoes
69. Keep a journal
70. Keep a sketchbook
71. Become computer literate
72. Meet an aboriginal painter
73. Read all of the books I own but have not read yet
74. Plant a cherry blossom tree
75. Visit my sister in Brazil
76. Re-decorate my home

77. Go on an archeological dig
78. Meet broadcaster Richard Fidler, and observe him interviewing someone in the studio
79. Master the art of meditation
80. Re-design my garden
81. Invent something
82. Cruise down the River Nile
83. Write a book the makes the New York Times best seller list
84. Create a you tube video
85. Go scuba diving
86. Spend a day with artist Judith Laws in her studio
87. Sail around the Greek Islands
88. Learn how to listen (see #78)
89. Have a massage once a week
90. Go rock climbing
91. Fly first class
92. Learn how to body surf properly
93. Drive an E-type Jag
94. Be part of a flash mob
95. Learn to dance the tango
96. Take up Qi Gong
97. Be an extra on a TV show
98. Donate a million dollars to charity
99. Visit the Maldives
100. Learn to dance the Viennese Waltz
101. Change at least one person's negative perception of mental illness

Because of bipolar life is hard but it can be rewarding too.

It all depends on your point of view.

It all depends on you.

The Viennese Waltz

One thing I would love to do is to learn the Viennese Waltz. Everyone dances. Dancing is such an affirmation of life. We all tap our toes and drum our fingers to music without even thinking about it, responding to something primeval within us.

My enthusiasm for dance far outweighs my ability, and I don't dance all that well. I do dance, but unfortunately, I don't have much style, elegance or talent.

Ballroom dancing is something I have tried in the past, but never mastered. I have watched others, and wished, with my heart and soul, that I could dance like them. Not like professional dancers, with their artificial poses and fixed smiles, but more like my elderly relatives, who, when they dance, are magically transformed into different people, transported to other places and times.

When the music starts, they assume their positions. She waits and he approaches her. Their bodies sway, their feet perform the steps and their shoulders stay fixed in the regal strains of the waltz. They become lost in motions beyond words and feelings, beyond logic.

They dance.

As they glide around the floor, she is secure within his embrace. They have incredible rapport, driven by their relationship, their experience and their shared passion for the dance. Their movements are assured, yet relaxed. They look happy.

I watch their feet, their bodies, their hands and their faces. I watch their eyes and their smiles. The upright way she holds herself as she moves around the floor. The formal way he holds her, his elbows high, one hand resting gently on her back. The way he leads and she responds. It is romance, music, art, high fashion, discipline, grace and exercise all in one.

I watch them as they dance the Viennese Waltz. I love this waltz. It is one of the oldest dances, dating back to the 12th and 13th centuries. It epitomises all the appeal of every ballroom dance – it has elegance and romance, class and style.

The Viennese Waltz contains the steps of a regular waltz, but includes dips and swings. Her dress moves in rhythm with her body, adding grace to her steps and excitement to her spins.

I want what she's having.

In that moment, I want to be her. I want to experience that life-affirming dance. I want to satisfy that primeval longing. I want to discover new pleasures and new aspects of myself and my life, but to do so I need to move past the barriers of inexperience, intimidation and frustration.

Is it ever too late to learn to dance?

I hope not, because I want to learn to dance the Viennese Waltz.

I want to have dancing lessons and I have decided who I want my teacher to be: Maksim Chmerkovskiy from America's *Dancing with the stars*. OK, he lives in America, but you never know. I could be in America and happen to be in the city where his dance studio is. I could walk in and he could just happen to be there ... and ...

Or, he could read my blog and be so impressed that I have expressed an interest in being his student and ... that he could offer to come to Australia ... and ...

I wish.

Life's full of surprises and, as I said, you never know.

Wouldn't it be exciting?

The dancer - Pencil on paper 410 x 590 mm

Epilogue

Not the South Pacific

It was not the South Pacific, it was The Great Barrier Reef. A tiny coral cay off Heron Island, near Gladstone in Queensland.

It was the perfect time of year. The skies were blue, the temperatures warm and the breezes were cool. The beach was stunning. During the day the mutton birds screeched and squawked and at night I could hear the waves gently lapping the shore.

Wilson Island only caters for twelve guests – six couples, plus a host and a chef. I went with my husband and ten of our closest friends. It is an eco-island and there are no modern conveniences. There is no electricity and food is cooked using gas cylinders.

You cannot use you phone, computer or hairdryer. When it gets dark you use tiny wind up torches to navigate your way from the dining table to your five star, open-air tent.

We had the whole island to ourselves, for three days and two nights.

My memories of Wilson Island are not fragmented at all. I remember everything clearly. Good things, like sumptuous food, comfortable lounges, leisurely walks and playing scrabble with my friends. Breathtaking things like orange sunsets and jet-black skies at night. Miracles of nature and ancient rituals. Life affirming things.

In awe and reverence I swam in pristine waters surrounded by unimaginable beauty. Translucent fish shimmered through the dazzling sunlight. The ocean teemed with life, and I saw magnificently coloured tropical fish, stingrays and coral.

One day I saw a dark shadow circling below. It was a reef shark. I raised my arm and signaled for one of my friends to come over and have a look.

I was waving, not drowning.

I have no unhappy memories of Wilson Island. There was isolation of course, but no disconnection, dislocation or disorientation. I was on my own when I wanted to be alone, but with my friends when I wanted company. My time there was idyllic.

They were, quite possibly, the best three days of my life.

Pristine waters - Acrylic on canvas 700 x 1000 mm

Part II:

Bipolar disorder

Information and advice for:

people who have bipolar disorder
carers and friends of people who have a mental illness and
anyone who is interested in mental health

Introduction to mental illness

'Mental health problems do not affect three or four out of every five persons, but one out of one.' William Menninger

How's your mental health?

Look at your own mental health.
If it's fine that's great,

lucky you.

But don't be complacent or condescending.

Don't think it can't happen to you
because it might.

It happens to all sorts of people,
you'd be surprised.

Maybe your mental health is not fine.
Maybe your husband or wife, son or daughter,
relative or friend, has bipolar disorder.

If they do, know that it is treatable
and it can be managed well.

There is a lot of help and support out there.

Rose-coloured glasses - Charcoal on paper 200 x 300

Everyone knows someone

'Friendship is born at that moment when one person says to another: 'What! You too? I thought I was the only one.' C S Lewis

Everyone knows someone, or knows someone who knows someone, who has, or who lives with, or is friends with, or works with, someone living with a mental illness, whether they know it or not.

If you have never thought about it, or don't believe you know anyone affected by mental illness, then you are either living in ignorance or denial.

Mental illness by nature is relative, subjective and contextual. At times we are all a little (or more than a little) crazy, although most of us are very good at hiding it. Who has never done anything inappropriate and out of character? Who has never felt really anxious, depressed or obsessed?

Who has never had a colleague with an obvious personality disorder? Isn't there one in every workplace? Maybe it's you.

We all have a thin veneer of normality, and if you scratch the surface, it's amazing what you find underneath.

I love it when I tell people I have bipolar disorder and they respond by telling me about their own anxieties, or the medication they take for depression, or their dependence on alcohol (not that drinking too much means you have a mental illness). They are relieved to be able to talk about it to someone who won't judge them.

When does 'normal' worrying about things become an anxiety disorder? At what point does feeling stressed tip into clinical depression? Just how many glasses of red wine after dinner every night are too many?

What's normal anyway? We can all find ourselves somewhere in the DSM IV (Diagnostic and Statistical Manual of Mental Disorders).

The great tragedy of mental illness is, of course, that people don't talk about it. They won't, or can't, speak openly or honestly about themselves, about their relatives, or even about family members from past generations.

It is too painful, too shameful and their fear of the possible consequences of disclosure is too terrifying.

I understand that it is difficult to talk about, but the greater tragedy and cost to our society is in not talking about it. We pay a very high price.

There is not a lot of understanding about mental illness in the community, so when people find out I have bipolar disorder, they often ask me a lot of questions.

- What exactly is it?
- What is a 'breakdown'?
- What actually happens?
- How can you recognise it?
- Who does it happen to and why?
- What is it like to have a mental illness?
- How do people deal with it and can they recover?
- If so, how do they recover?
- What can I do if it happens to someone I care about?

There are four important facts I believe everyone should know about mental illness.

Fact #1

It can't be explained easily. It's a bit like childbirth. You read everything you can get your hands on, talk to everyone you meet, go to classes, prepare as much as you can and think you have a handle on it.

But when it happens, it blows you out of the water, and you realise that you had understood very little of what it would be like to give birth, or to have a baby.

Your whole world is irrevocably transformed, for better and for worse. The conundrum, of course, is that it's almost impossible to explain what is like to anyone who hasn't been through it themselves.

Mental illness is a bit like that, except you don't get a baby at the end. Well ... not unless you've been manic, and slept with someone without taking precautions ...

Fact #2

It is very difficult to explain what it is like to have a mental illness, and impossible to do so in the course of one conversation.

It is relatively easy to discuss mental illness in academic terms, however articulating a 'lived experience' is another thing altogether. A person's experience of mental illness cannot be told easily or quickly. Besides, one story is only a part of that person's whole experience, and you need to hear some of their other stories to put it into context.

Fact #3

There are multiple facets to mental illness. Just like childbirth and parenthood, there are many perspectives and points of view. It's not all good and it's not all bad.

There are endings and beginnings, and beginnings and endings. One thing is certain, after you experience it, your life will never be the same again.

Fact #4

The impact of mental illness is different for everyone (which is not to say we don't all have a lot of things in common). Every person who has a mental illness (or is the carer of someone who does) has their own unique story, and people with the same disorder experience it differently. Mental illness, in all its forms, is not fixed, but fluid, with continually shifting boundaries and borders.

Everyone knows someone - Oil on canvas 460 x 460 mm

Definitions and statistics

As I said, this is not an information text about mental illness and bipolar disorder, it is a book of personal stories. However, it may be helpful to explain a few things, so you will have some idea of what I am talking about as you continue reading. These are my own definitions of the terms, as I understand them.

Mental illness: An illness, diagnosed by a doctor, in accordance with specific medical diagnostic guidelines. It is a general term that covers a variety of conditions including (but not limited to) depression, bipolar disorder, schizophrenia, PTSD (post-traumatic stress disorder) personality disorders and eating disorders.

Bipolar I: A medically diagnosed disorder, comprising episodes of mania and depression. It is characterised by extreme changes in mood, over a period of weeks or months. It may involve psychosis and the need for hospitalization.

Bipolar II: A medically diagnosed disorder comprising mainly recurrent depression with episodes of hypomania, but not mania (see below). Some people believe that *a)* bipolar II doesn't really exist, *b)* it is a mild disorder or *c)* it doesn't require medication. Each person diagnosed with bipolar II is different, and for some *b* and *c* are true. However many (or most) people with bipolar II experience it as more severe than a mild disorder and they do require medication. It is naïve to underestimate the damage that untreated bipolar II can do.

Mania: Symptoms include elevated mood, increased energy and activity, less need for sleep, irritability, rapid speech and grandiose ideas. It may involve psychosis and often requires hospitalisation.

Hypomania: This is a less severe form of mania, which does not impair daily functioning as much as mania. It is not accompanied by psychosis and there is usually no need for hospitalisation.

Psychosis: This is characterised by an inability to distinguish what is real and what is not real. The person's understanding of reality is either lost or distorted and they have hallucinations or delusions.

Clinical depression: This is a depressed mood that significantly impacts on a person's mental, emotional or social life. Symptoms can include extreme lethargy, indecisiveness, and feelings of worthlessness and guilt. The person can have suicidal thoughts and may attempt to take their own life. Clinical depression is different from depression that can occur after a loss or difficult life experience.

ECT (Electroconvulsive Therapy): This treatment involves an electrical current being briefly applied to the brain under anaesthetic, and is used to treat severe depression. It does have side effects, but is said to be painless, safe and effective. It may be life saving for people at high risk of suicide.

ADHD (Attention Deficit Hyperactivity Disorder): This disorder is associated with inattention, hyperactivity and impulsivity. To be diagnosed with ADHD, you must have had the symptoms since childhood.

Bipolar disorder is a neurobiological condition that causes abnormalities in the structure and the function of the brain. No one really knows what causes it, but genes are definitely involved. In my understanding, there is little evidence to show it is caused by environmental factors, and although stress and difficult life events may trigger bipolar disorder, or exacerbate it, they don't cause it.

Consumers

Consumer (noun): 1. A person who purchases goods and services for personal use.

When I found out I had bipolar disorder I became part of a group called *'consumers'*. The term *'consumer'* is used by mental health professionals and academics to refer to people like me, but isn't everyone a consumer?

Personally, I think categorising people who have a mental illness *'consumers'* is stupid. Anyway, I don't consume the services of mental health professionals, I employ them. It is only a slight distinction but, to me anyway, it is an important one. I feel strongly about it, but other people may think differently.

When mental health professionals and academics are referring to *me*, guess which of the following I would prefer:

1. This is Anne.

2. This is Anne. She has bipolar disorder.

3. This is Anne. She is a consumer.

Correct.

Number 1, followed by number 2 and not number 3.

My doctor can call me a patient. My psychologist can call me a client. My pharmacist can call me a customer. Everyone else can just call me Anne.

About bipolar

One in five

According to the Black Dog Institute website (www. blackdoginstitute.org.au):

- "One in five Australians experiences a mental illness within a 12-month period.

- In 2007, almost half (45%) of all Australians had experienced a mental disorder at some point in their lifetime.

- Mental disorders are the third leading cause of the non-fatal burden of disease and injury in Australia.

- The World Health Organisation estimates that depression will be the number one cause of disability in both the developed and developing worlds by 2030.

- Findings of a 2007 Australian National Survey of Mental Health & Wellbeing about bipolar disorder:

  - Life-time prevalence is 1.3%

  - 12-month prevalence is 0.9%.

- A 2005 US community epidemiological study (the National Epidemiologic Survey on Alcohol and Related Conditions), estimated the lifetime risk of bipolar I and bipolar II as ranging from 3-10%.

- The odds of developing bipolar I disorder appear to be greatest for people in the 18-29 year age group, with odds decreasing in age

- The financial costs of bipolar disorder to the Australian community amount to $1.59 billion per annum through inability to function at home and in the workplace.

- The causes of bipolar disorder are approximately 50% attributable to genes and 50% to environmental factors.

- Of all Australians with bipolar disorder, only one-third receive treatment, 40% are not taking medication and only 17% access adjunctive psychosocial rehabilitation programs.

- On average, 69% of people with bipolar disorder are misdiagnosed 3.5 times. On average, it takes 10.2 years and 4 doctors to obtain a correct diagnosis of bipolar disorder."

The good news

The good news is that bipolar disorder is eminently treatable. Individuals, families and friends can do a lot to make sure that the light at the end of the tunnel is bright sunshine and not the headlights of an oncoming train. The chances of a train wreck increase significantly when you do nothing about it, and just stand frozen in place.

There are many 'good news' stories about bipolar disorder, including mine. Many of us are living with bipolar disorder and other forms of mental illness and coping very well. You just don't know who we are. We could be your child's teacher, your GP, your lawyer, your electrician, your mechanic or your newsagent. We could be anyone. Most people in the community who live well with bipolar don't advertise the fact. We just get on with our lives.

Given community perceptions, you could be forgiven for thinking that everything to do with mental illness and bipolar disorder is morbid and sad, but in actual fact it's not. Having bipolar disorder can enhance motivation, increase productivity and lead to innovation in all areas of life. It can, and does, stimulate imagination and creativity in many people both in history and in contemporary society.

I read somewhere that people who have a mental illness are often the creative and innovative minds of the world. We are people who look at things differently. We often have great lateral thinking skills. We have enthusiasm and spirit (when we are not depressed) and we have a great ability to relate to other people, especially others who face challenges in their lives.

Because of bipolar you win

What you lose on the merry-go-round, you gain on the swings.

Like many people who have gone through difficult experiences, my priorities have changed. I have become more philosophical less worried about things that don't really matter and more focused on the things that really do matter. What matters to me are my husband, my family and my close friends.

So, what do you really gain?

I believe you gain:

- understanding of many things
- compassion and empathy
- acceptance of yourself and of others who are different
- new social supports (if you're lucky)
- an opportunity to work in different ways
- the discovery of new talents
- and most exciting of all, the opportunity to re-invent yourself.

The bad news

Bipolar disorder has a positive side, but at the same time it can be devastating. I don't want to minimise the havoc it can wreak. I have seen the destruction, desolation and despair at first hand.

If you have bipolar disorder it affects every aspect of your life, including your physical health, cognitive skills, social skills, emotional wellbeing, finances and relationships.

The impact of bipolar disorder varies from person to person, and episodes range from mild and infrequent, to severe and chronic. It is a complex condition for which there is no cure.

Bipolar disorder is life long, episodic, and it can recur frequently, despite strict compliance with medical treatment and/or medication. There are also comorbid (coexisting) conditions such as anxiety and alcohol and substance abuse. People who have bipolar disorder also have a significantly increased risk of suicide.

How you treat bipolar disorder, and learn to live with it, is with ongoing psychiatric treatment and/or lifelong medication, psychological support, and diet, exercise, meditation and whatever else you think helps.

I believe that trying to treat bipolar disorder without medication is risky at best and catastrophic at worst, but that's just my opinion, and as I said, I am not a doctor. What is not disputed though is that getting a correct diagnosis can, and usually does, take many years. Around two-thirds of people are initially given at least one incorrect diagnosis, before getting the right one.

People who have little first-hand experience of bipolar disorder usually have great difficulty comprehending it. Ignorance is widespread, and disordered behavior associated with mental illness is seen by many as a matter of choice rather than an involuntary condition. There is a widespread perception that a person who is mentally ill just needs to pull themselves together, and exercise some self-control.

That's simply not true.

Because of bipolar you lose

Because of bipolar you lose a lot. Researchers tell us that more than half of people with bipolar disorder manifest cognitive dysfunction (difficulties with thinking) at some time and to some extent. This impacts on the person's day to day functioning to a greater or lesser degree and can cause problems with problem solving, logical reasoning, language, memory, planning and organizational abilities, flexibility, inhibition and dis-inhibition responses, visual spatial function such as map reading, the capacity for empathy and IQ.

That's all well and good, but what do these things really mean? They don't mean a lot to me, as a person trying my best to live with bipolar disorder. They do indicate, though, that there is a lot of jargon in the world of psychiatry.

So, what do you really lose?

I believe you lose:

- your understanding of yourself and the life you have already lived
- your identity as a 'normal' person
- the perception that your life is perfect, or at least could be perfect
- your identity (now you're not the same as you were before)
- your sense of self (who you feel you are)
- friends (some, many or most of them)
- your confidence as a human being
- pride in yourself, as the consummate professional you once were
- your ability to work as you once did. Feeling good or at least OK
- security in your relationships (pretty much all of them)
- a medication free life (probably forever)
- your previous expectations that your life would be 'normal' whatever that means
- your ability to do things as well as you could before
- your ability to concentration, remember and be alert
- and most of all your ability to live the rest of your life without fear of relapse.

Sometimes I worry about it all. I can deny it and I can fight it. On the other hand I can also embrace it and choose to enjoy the positive side.

A heavy load - Charcoal on paper 400 x 600 mm

Anxiety

Bipolar's best friend, anxiety

Do you sometimes have:

- buzzing in your ears
- tightness in your chest
- indigestion
- dizziness
- bad backache for no reason
- headaches
- muscle aches and pains
- sweating
- nausea
- shaking hands
- the feeling that you might faint
- the feeling that you're having a heart attack (seriously)
- heart palpitations
- breathing difficulties
- sweating
- tingling
- increased heart rate
- raised blood pressure
- dry mouth
- butterflies in your stomach
- irritability
- sleep problems
- a desperate, physical urge to escape from stressful situations, such as large groups or social events?

Well ... you could be very ill, or dying. Then again, maybe you've met bipolar's best friend, anxiety.

Question: What should you do?

Answer: Drink a lot of coffee, take up smoking and drink alcohol. Eat yummy fried food, McDonalds, KFC, Twisties, Cornettos, chips and chocolate bars. Relax by watching a lot of TV: *The biggest loser* and the *The fat family diet* (they will make you feel much better about yourself). Don't exercise - that will only lead to muscle strains and injuries. Avoid socialising.

Sound tempting? It's what I do (sometimes I can't help it and I love it).

Unfortunately, according to medical advice, these are not the answers. Apparently they can decrease your anxiety for a short time, but they will make it worse in the long run. So, what can you do? Seriously.

- Research it.
- Learn to recognise it for what it is.
- Talk to other people who have too.
- Live with it.
- See your doctor.
- Look at behaviour therapy.
- Try cognitive behaviour therapy.
- Consider psychotherapy.
- Investigate support groups.
- Ask about medication.
- Think about your diet, exercise and lifestyle.

Personally, I try to live with it. I don't often go to a support group, but I do get very excited when I meet someone else who hangs out with bipolar's best friend too.

These days, I am stable, well and happy but anxiety is always with me, hovering in the background.

When I say something slightly inappropriate or do something a bit odd, I worry that other people think, '*She's a little bit weird.'* But it is done and I can't go back and unsay it or undo it. Trying to explain only makes it worse. Then paranoia joins the party (*Oh my god, they're all looking at me, I just know they're talking about me*).

It may be paranoia, but it may not. If I have said something a little off, been a little too intense, flown off the handle over something small or behaved a bit strangely, they probably ARE talking about me. Are they? I don't know.

In comes obsession and rumination.

And let's not get started on OCD.

Gambling, drinking and drug taking

Love the pokies?

Do you love the pokies?

   I do (but I try to stay away from them).

   So do a lot of people with (and without) bipolar disorder.

A few months ago, one Saturday morning, I went to a meeting at my local club. The meeting started at 9.00am and I arrived at ten to nine. As I approached the club, I saw a long queue of people snaking down the street and around the corner. Most of them were elderly.

   I entered the club by a side door to bypass the queue. As I signed the attendance sheet, I asked the lady at the reception desk why all the people were lined up outside, and she said that they were waiting for the club to open so that they could come in and play the poker machines.

   My meeting finished about an hour and a half later, and on my way out I saw that the poker machine area was more than half full of people playing the machines.

   'Bet with your head not over it,' said a small sign on the wall beside the cashier.

   But that's the problem isn't it. If your head's not in the right place, or if you're not right in the head, then of course you're going to bet over it.

   People with bipolar disorder who gamble can, and often do, accrue large debts. They lose their homes or misappropriate money. They suffer from depression, stress, lethargy, insomnia, poor nutrition, suicidal thoughts, and increased caffeine and nicotine consumption.

   Gambling has a symbiotic relationship with mental illness and it can be a symptom of depression. In a Flinders University study in 2006, they surveyed 79 people with a gambling problem over 1 year. Of these, 81.4% had showed some suicidal ideation (thoughts) and 30.2% had reported one or more suicide attempts in the preceding 12 months.

Addiction to poker machines can destroy people's lives. 300,000 Australians have a gambling problem (to some degree). For every gambler, between 5 and 10 others (partners and children) are affected. To these people, poker machines are not just a form of recreation.

You could substitute the word 'gambling' for 'alcohol' or 'drugs' and much of the above would apply.

These problems are complex and it is really hard (if not impossible) to sort them out on your own. Whether you have bipolar disorder or not, if gambling, drinking and/or taking drugs are a problem for you, don't stick your head in the sand.

Get some help. The sooner the better.

One for the road - Charcoal on paper 200 x 300 mm

Diagnosis and treatment

Getting a diagnosis

Once you have it, the suspicion that something is wrong, the lid is off Pandora's Box and there's no way of putting it back on. Ignorance is not always bliss. You can pretend it isn't happening, but denial will not make it go away.

The best course of action (in my opinion) is to face up to it, go to the doctor, get a referral to a specialist and get a definitive diagnosis. Then you'll know one way or the other.

It may not be what you think it is. You may not have lost your mind.

But if it is, and you find out you are mentally ill, or you have bipolar disorder, get treatment and help from a professional.

If (after you have seen someone) you feel worse, go back and talk to them. If you are prescribed medication, and you don't want to take it, go back and talk to them. If you take medication and you have side effects that you can't handle, go back and talk to them.

And if you start to feel really well or really, really (really) well, go back and talk to them straight away.

When you have bipolar disorder, too much of anything is not a good thing.

Among friends - Oil pastel on paper 250 x 270 mm

Medication

Approximately forty percent of people who have bipolar disorder take three or more psychotropic medications and eighteen percent take four or more.

Having to take medication is the pits. Who would want to take it in the first place, let alone deal with the side effects, keep track of it all, remember to get the scripts and pay through the nose for the privilege?

Then, after all that, you have to make sure you don't forget to take when you're supposed to. All of this when you have trouble with your memory. Seriously, it's not easy. It seems to me that psychiatrists fly blind when it comes to knowing and advising which medications you should take, in what doses and for how long.

Everyone is different, the presentation of their illness is different, and treatment is too. It is pure guesswork a lot of the time. Also, what gets you well does not necessarily keep you well. You have to keep modifying your medication as your symptoms change, although this doesn't happen as often or as much after the first few years.

The side effects of medication are also different for everyone and they cannot really be predicted, except in my case. I seem to get almost all of those so helpfully listed on the information sheets from the drug companies.

Getting fat, for example, really, really fat, is not fun. In a frighteningly short period of time on a new medication you can look like you are nine months pregnant, feel like a zombie and experience the delights of such things as severe constipation and nausea. On other medication you can get Parkinson's-like tremors where your hands can't stop shaking.

Then there is the lack of mental acuity (from the illness, or the meds, or both) which means you're not as smart as you used to be. 'A few fries short of a happy meal', I heard someone say once. A happy meal that you shouldn't be eating, in an attempt to lose some of the weight you have put on. You know it and it's obvious to everyone around you.

All of it is hard to swallow, but take your medication and be grateful. It's not such a high price to pay for the promise (or hope) of sanity. Is it? No, it isn't.

I would, and I do, choose sanity over side effects every day.

Potential side effects of the medications I take (common and rare) according to the consumer medicine information provided by the pharmaceutical companies include:

Medication # 1

Fatal skin rash, dizziness/unsteadiness, headache, drowsiness, nausea, vomiting, weakness, double vision, blurred vision, tremor, trouble sleeping, loss of memory, confusion irritability/ aggression, agitation and joint/back pain.

Medication # 2

Feeling sleepy, feeling dizzy or faint, feeling weak, constipation, dry mouth, runny or stuffy nose, indigestion, fainting, uncontrolled movements of the tongue, mouth, cheeks or jaws, sudden increase in body temperature with sweating or fast heartbeat, very fast breathing, muscle stiffness, restless leg syndrome and seizures.

Medication #3

Hand tremors, thirst, nausea, allergic reactions (rash, hives, difficulty breathing, tightness in chest swelling of the mouth, face, lips or tongue), blurred vision, confusion, diarrhea, drowsiness, excessive weight gain, giddiness, inability to control the bladder or bowels, increased thirst, increased or decreased urination, involuntary twitching or muscle movements, loss of coordination, muscle weakness, persistent headache, persistent or severe nausea, ringing in the ears, seizures, slow or irregular heartbeat, slurred speech, swelling of the ankles or wrists, unsteadiness, vision changes and vomiting.

In taking these medications I have (luckily) missed out on the fatal skin rash. I have also managed to avoid the uncontrollable movements of the tongue, mouth, cheeks or jaws (so far), although I am told that this may occur some years down the track, and if it does, it could be permanent. I have not, however, missed out on the delights of:

Akathisia (a very distressing movement disorder), dizziness, headaches, drowsiness, nausea, weakness, blurred vision, hand tremor, trouble sleeping, memory loss, confusion, irritability/aggression, agitation, joint/back pain, feeling sleepy, feeling dizzy or faint, feeling weak, constipation, dry mouth, stuffy nose, indigestion, muscle stiffness, restless leg syndrome, seizures (one), thirst, allergic reactions (rash, hives and itching), diarrhea, weight gain, tinnitus, laryngeal dystonia (spasm of the throat that can cause choking on food).

Some of these side effects have been fleeting and some have occurred only once or twice. Others, however, have been more persistent and pervasive. I don't experience unpleasant side effects all of the time but I do often enough for them to be a pain in my increasingly large bottom, speaking of which...

In the eye of the beholder - Oil on canvas 700 x 1000 mm

The side of a house (and how not to look like one)

If I was planning to read this book (and hadn't yet done so), the first thing I would do, after looking at the contents page, would be to come straight to this chapter. You see, I am obsessed with mental illness, medication and weight gain.

Nothing destroys your self-esteem more than being transformed from a person who is a normal weight (or, OK, slightly overweight) to a person who is considerably overweight. A psychiatrist I met once told me that a patient had said to her, "There is only one thing worse than being mentally ill, and that is being mentally ill and fat."

That really resonated with me.

There is a derogatory expression that says if you are fat, you look like the side of a house. I certainly feel like one most of the time, despite trying to exercise and watch what I eat. It's the meds. Even on very small doses, I have, at times, an overwhelming compulsion to EAT, EAT, EAT.

A few months ago, I went through a stage where I would wake up through the night to eat. Every single night. It was weird. A feeling of starvation would wake me suddenly from a very deep sleep. I absolutely had to eat, straight away. I would stagger out of bed on autopilot and go into the kitchen, more than half asleep, still drugged from the medication I had taken before bedtime.

I would scavenge whatever I could find, and then go back to bed and back to sleep, or I would bring food into the bed with me and eat it with my eyes closed, sometimes eating lying down. An hour later it would happen again. Two hours after that it would happen again.

Sleep is key when you have bipolar disorder. I have heard a (tongue in cheek) suggestion, that bipolar could, in the future, be classified as a sleep disorder. I think that's very perceptive. It is not primarily a sleep disorder, but I digress. Anyway ...

... I wouldn't be able to get back to sleep so I would go and sit in the lounge room and watch TV for an hour. Then I would go back to bed and sleep for the remaining hours until morning. I would have eaten two, three or four snacks through the night. This went on for months, and still happens sometimes.

I know what you might think. It is NOT just a matter of self-control, and it hasn't only happened to me. Lots of people with mental illness put on weight. It comes with the territory in the world of psychotropic medications.

In the end, I changed one of my meds. The night-time eating stopped straight away (although it did make another appearance recently) and so did a lot of other side effects (some that I didn't even realise were side effects). I still take medication that causes weight gain in some people, but I am not raiding the fridge at night *quite* as much.

Lots of people without mental illness put on weight too, and even though I struggle with my weight, many of my friends (who are not on psychotropic meds) do as well. So, maybe it's not the meds to blame for my weight gain. Maybe it is age, hormones or simply eating too much.

How do you circumvent weight gain on psychotropic meds? In my experience, you have three options:

Exercise and diet (I know what you are thinking, and I whole-heartedly agree).

Accept it, and yourself, just the way you are (I know what you are thinking, and I whole-heartedly agree).

Change your meds, if you can get your psychiatrist's consent (I know what your psychiatrist will probably think, but have a go anyway).

I have done a lot of reading and research into all of this, and I could talk at length about the pros and cons of each of these three options: the difficulties, and whether or not they can or can't, do or don't, will or won't work. In the end it all boils down to this:

Question: How do people lose weight on meds?
Answer: They find it very difficult.

Question: How do people lose weight when they're not on meds?
Answer: They find it very difficult.

If I really had the answers, this would be a very different book, and I would be rich.

I wish.

Beautiful curves - Pencil and charcoal on paper 600 x 430 mm

The drug companies

Drug companies get bad press. Medications get criticised. This is true in all areas of health, but more so in the area of mental health. All the negative and challenging things I have said about taking psychotropic medications are true (for me). But the greater truth is that medications can, and do, save lives. They also make a huge difference to the quality of life for many, many people suffering from bipolar disorder, schizophrenia, depression and many other mental disorders.

I am extremely grateful to drug companies for enabling me to have access to the medications I take, and I am also grateful to the government for subsidising (some of) them. Drug companies not only provide medication and undertake and fund research, they educate medical professionals and the wider community. They offer research grants, prizes and awards to people who are passionate about working to improve the lives of those with bipolar disorder, to doctors and researchers who devote their entire professional lives to this pursuit.

When I was in the early stages of my illness, and searching for information, I found out about an international scientific conference on bipolar disorder (The Australasian Society for Bipolar and Depressive Disorders Conference). It was primarily for doctors and researchers but anyone could to attend.

At this conference I met some very interesting and interested people including my (wonderful, empathetic, knowledgeable and insightful) future psychiatrist. Attending this conference was incredibly empowering. The information was 'cutting edge' and fascinating. I was among doctors, academics and researchers, men and women who were committed to improving the lives of people with bipolar disorder.

Some of the sessions were sponsored by drug companies, such as Janssen-Cilag, AstraZeneca, Eli Lilly, Wyeth, Pfizer and others. Conference participants who were not medical professionals were asked not to go into the area where the drug companies were promoting their products, so of course I did. I looked at all their literature and information. I talked to their representatives and I collected a few things like pens and note pads.

Actually, I took three or four A4 note books, a set of headphones, a hole punch, a sticky tape dispenser, lots of pens, a pedometer, post it notes, mints, 6 postcards, and lots of other things I can't remember. It was great fun. I still drink out of my prized Seroquel coffee mug. That conference was a few years ago now and I don't think that drug companies are allowed to hand out marketing 'freebies' any more. Shame.

Three generations ago, in my grandparent's day, today's medications were (obviously) not available. There was no lithium and there were no mood stabilisers. The only treatments for severe, intractable depression were ECT and lobotomies. Would this be my fate today if the drugs I take were unavailable? Would I be living out the rest of my life in and out of psychiatric institutions? I believe that it is thanks to my medication that I function so well, can work productively and am able to contribute to my family and to society. My life, and the lives of my husband and children, would not be the same without it.

It took a lot of time to find the mix of medications that work best for me (both the types of medications and the dosages), but today I am doing well and I am inordinately grateful for the medications that ameliorate the worst effects of what is a severely debilitating illness.

Shocking treatment

Shock treatment (electroconvulsive therapy) has bad press. Images from the early 20th century and from movies such as *One flew over the Cuckoo's Nest* are burned into our individual and collective consciousness, and this has meant the there is a very negative perception of ECT.

On the face of it, the treatment for very intractable depression doesn't seem to have changed since the 1950s. Shock treatment is still used today, and is the preferred treatment for severely (and I mean severely) depressed patients who are suicidal. I haven't had ECT, but I know others who have.

If you are deemed to require ECT, you will (potentially) undertake a course of six to eight treatments within a time span of two weeks, every second day. Each time you will be given a general anaesthetic, and electrodes will be attached to either side of your head, and sometimes in the middle of your forehead as well.

Then you will be zapped with an electric current, which will cause a seizure (that's the convulsive part of ECT – electro convulsive therapy). Afterwards the nursing staff will tape a piece of paper to your bedside table with your name on it and what day it is, because when you come around you won't be able to remember them.

Afterwards, your jaw will be sore from clenching your teeth. You might have bitten your tongue or lip. Unsurprisingly, you'll probably have a headache. Your memory will have disappeared and your mood might not improve much afterwards anyway.

The day after treatment will be bad, but later you won't remember just how bad it was, because of your memory loss. The doctor's explanation for any lack of improvement will be that you haven't had enough treatments yet.

Recent studies of electroconvulsive therapy (ECT) have found that the treatment is effective in relieving depression, and it is suggested that in some cases it may be more effective than medication. Memory loss is the biggest problem.

They say ECT is life saving for some, and it is.

If you need it, you need it.

Attitudes towards mental illness

If it looks like a duck

If it looks like a duck, swims like a duck, and quacks like a duck, then it probably *is* a duck. But it might not be. Until you know something for sure, you should assume nothing.

If you have bipolar disorder, don't make assumptions about yourself. If you know someone with bipolar disorder, don't make assumptions about them either.

If you don't (think you) know anyone with bipolar disorder, be extra careful, especially if you meet someone you get on really well with, someone just like you.

They probably are just like you.

But you might be wrong or you might have only part of the story.

You might also be wrong about yourself. Maybe you're the one who is a duck. Or not. But by making assumptions, you might be a goose.

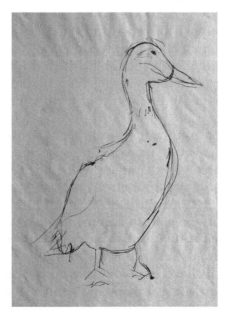

If it looks like a duck - Ink on paper 600 x 760 mm

Anonymity

One of the hardest things about having a mental illness is disclosure, particularly in the workplace. I understand that it can (theoretically) be positive and helpful to tell others about it, but I know that it can also be disastrous, leaving people unsupported and exposed to stigma and discrimination.

There is no statutory obligation for a person to disclose that they have a mental illness to a current employer, or to a prospective one. You only need to do so if it will interfere with your performance at work or if there is a safety risk to yourself or to anyone you work with.

However, when applying for some jobs it appears that disclosure is unavoidable. Take, for example, the following question in the declaration section of an application form for a job in a large state government organisation:

Are you aware of any illness, disability or condition which might interfere with your ability to perform the full range of [the] duties [associated with this position]?
Answer Yes or No ...
Note: If you answered Yes ... please send full details to...

If you have bipolar disorder, and do not wish to disclose it (as is your legal right), this is a very difficult question to answer. *Yes* is the strictly accurate response, as (yes) you are aware that you have bipolar disorder, and (yes) it is a condition that *might* (possibly, potentially or hypothetically, at some time in the future) interfere with your ability to perform the full range of duties of the job. But answering *Yes* is in direct conflict with your legal right not to disclose your mental illness to a future employer.

Let's say, for argument's sake, that at the time you apply for this position, your mental illness is under control and has been for some years. You are well, and there is no reason to think this will not continue. You visit your psychiatrist regularly and they monitor the state of your mental health very carefully. If you start to become unwell, your doctor will adjust your medication and/or advise you on (lifestyle and other) strategies that will keep you healthy.

You do not believe that your mental illness will interfere with your performance at work and neither does your doctor.

146

Your bipolar disorder is managed very well and there is no risk to yourself, your colleagues or your clients.

After a lot of thought, consideration, and consultation with your specialist, you finally decide to tick *No* on your application form. You get the job. Your employer and colleagues do not know that you have bipolar disorder and you do not tell them as you do not believe it is either appropriate or necessary.

You are relieved because you think that if your colleagues knew you had bipolar disorder, they would feel differently about you, and would change the way they interacted with you. Or you would feel awkward and change the way you interacted with them. You are concerned that if you had a difference of opinion, or an argument with someone at work, they would use their knowledge of your mental illness against you. You fear that if your clients found out they would be unhappy that a person with a mental illness was acting for them or working on their behalf.

It's complicated. Some people with bipolar disorder can undertake their employment in a professional and competent manner. Others, however, cannot. As with many things in life, this issue is not black and white. People with mental illness and employment coexist in shades of grey.

A number of people with bipolar disorder are unable to work at all due to their condition. Some can work part time and others periodically. Many people have difficulties at work prior to diagnosis and treatment, but they can work without any problems afterwards.

Countless people with bipolar disorder thrive in the workplace and are extremely professional, productive, creative, hard-working and valued employees.

Some time ago, a NSW magistrate was deemed unfit to work by the Judicial Commission because of his (subsequently treated and stable) bipolar disorder. It was reported that although his judicial decisions were not in question, he had acted in a manner unbecoming to a judicial officer. He was required to argue his case before parliament in order to retain his job and politicians ultimately decided his fate.

Some newspaper editorials were impartial, some supportive of him and others scathing. In one editorial, comments were made that the magistrate was 'using the bipolar defence', and 'pleading the mental health card'.

People wrote letters to the editor arguing that those with bipolar disorder should not work in jobs where they are in control of people's lives, regardless of whether or not they are being treated successfully for their respective conditions. They said that this magistrate should not be allowed to continue to sit on the bench. Their reasoning was that people in such positions, who have a mental illness, successfully treated or not, cannot be fully capable of discharging their responsibilities, as there will always be the risk that they might not take their medication, or that their medication might not be effective.

A close family friend was a surgeon. At one stage, he had been feeling tired and unwell for some time, increasingly unable to work with his normal efficiency. There was no suggestion that his surgical skills were affected, however, his bedside manner at times was erratic. One day in the middle of an operation, he had a massive heart attack. No one accused him of 'pleading the heart attack card' to excuse his work difficulties prior to his heart attack. No one suggested that he shouldn't return to work once he had recovered, in case he wasn't taking his medication, the medication wasn't working, or he had another heart attack.

Naturally there must be checks and balances in place to ensure that people like magistrates and surgeons are competent and able to do their jobs. Of course systems need to be well regulated. Support should be provided when things go wrong and, of course, disciplinary action taken when someone's conduct is unacceptable.

I certainly do not want to appear before a judge who treats me unfairly because they are not thinking clearly, whether they have a mood disorder or not. I do not want to be in a plane flown by a pilot who is psychotic or even just strung out on too much caffeine and adrenaline. I do not want my child to be taught by someone who is mentally unstable for whatever reason.

That said, what would you do if you were a (capable and fair) magistrate, or a highly competent doctor, or pilot, or policeman or teacher (or anyone), and you suspected, or knew, that you had a mental illness? What if you knew you were very good at your job and had the respect of those you worked with? Would you think twice about seeking help if you thought you might lose your job because of it? Or lose your reputation? Or not actually get a job because of it? And if you did have a diagnosis of bipolar disorder, and it was being treated successfully, would you be reluctant to disclose the fact to anyone in your workplace or your community? Would you be worried about discrimination?

One day I was at work, in my (still newish) job, chatting happily to one of my colleagues. I had not disclosed to her (or anyone) that I had bipolar disorder. The workday had finished, and we were having a chat, talking about everything from our careers to our personal lives.

When I started working there, this colleague had been extremely helpful. She had explained everything, from where the toilets were, to how to access the intranet. Nothing was too much trouble, and she went out of her way to help me in any way she could. She was lovely, not only to me, but to everyone she interacted with.

This particular afternoon we were talking about news and current affairs. She was showing me an article in the newspaper, when I saw another, on the same page, about the magistrate mentioned above.

I said to my colleague, 'Look at that article. I wonder what the outcome was?'

She replied firmly and forcefully, 'I don't think those types of people should be in positions like that. You know what they're like. They never take their medication and you could never be sure that they wouldn't … '

She continued, clearly unaware that I was one of those 'types of people'. I am sure she wouldn't have said what she did if she had known. I didn't hear much of what she said after that. I felt like I had been punched. King hit out of nowhere. My face flushed, I felt hot and shaky and thought I was going to be sick.

Maybe what she said wasn't such a big deal, and maybe I over-reacted, but I do think her views are indicative of what many people think.

In any work place, the person with the mental illness (like me) usually looks and acts the same as everyone else (like her), and because they (people like me) are not visible, it perpetuates the stereotypes that people with mental illnesses are different (odd, strange and untrustworthy, to be feared and looked down upon) and look different.

After this encounter, I was totally convinced of one thing. I wasn't going to be telling anyone at work about having bipolar disorder in a hurry.

Another day a friend of mine (who is a social worker) was in a meeting with a number of colleagues discussing a client. My friend had met this client on a number of occasions and had liked her a lot. In the meeting, comments were made about the client's:

- (poor) mental health
- (obvious lack of) intelligence
- (unfortunate) socioeconomic background
- employment (as a cleaner)
- (filthy) living conditions
- (unsavoury) relatives in jail
- (dreadful) parenting skills
- and (total lack of) life skills.

The tone of the discussion was not derogatory at all. On the contrary, everyone was very respectful and supportive of the client, trying to work out how they could best support her.

Nevertheless …

How many people think that mental illness naturally coexists with: a low IQ, drug and alcohol problems, a dirty house, bad parenting, not coping and having unsavoury relatives?

How many people think that mental illness naturally coexists with: creativity, a high IQ, an immaculate house, tertiary qualifications, professional employment and excellent parenting?

I know what I think. What do you think?

Truly?

Some people make generalisations based on stereotypes and others don't, but how do you know who thinks what?

That's right, you don't.

'Mental illness is nothing to be ashamed of, but stigma and bias shame us all.' Bill Clinton

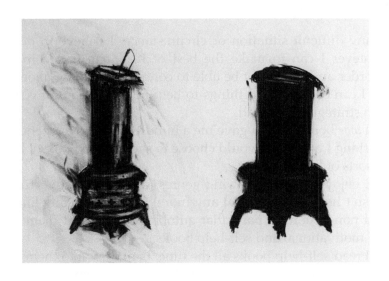

What, you too? - Charcoal on paper 600 x 430 mm

Self help

Self-help books

In any difficult situation or circumstance, I believe in doing whatever I can to make the best of it. I may have bipolar disorder and I may not be able to control everything about it, but I can choose to do things to help myself. One of my self-help strategies is to read.

I *love* books. If you gave me a hundred dollars to spend on anything I wanted, I would choose to spend it on books. I love all sorts of books.

I enjoy fiction of varying genres (although, sadly, erotica doesn't hold much appeal any more) and I also really like to read non-fiction, in particular autobiographies and memoirs, and motivational and self-help books.

I read self-help books all the time; I am drawn to them like a moth to a flame. Sadly though, they never seem to radically change my life. I read books with titles such as:

The ten habits of highly successful people
I have the secret
Ultimate happiness
Feel the fear and persevere regardless
Imagine yourself rich and how to turn the dream into reality
The seven secrets of slim people and so on.

These books promise to change my life. They assure me, if I follow their clear, straightforward and easy suggestions, I will be a better person. Stronger, fitter, richer and wiser.

However, I would like to see some self-help books with titles such as:

The seven habits of ordinary people
There is no secret
Happiness isn't everything
Feel the fear and try something else
Money isn't the answer
The seven secrets of people who don't care about their weight

152

Here are a few more suggestions of titles of books I would really like to read (maybe I should write them):

The cookbook for people who hate cooking
The secrets of getting out of bed in the morning when you don't want to go to work.
How to make sure that everyone in your family receives fabulous expensive looking birthday and Christmas cards/presents from you (before the due date, for under $10)
How to get the kids to feed and walk the dog and keep their rooms clean
100 ways to waste time

I think these self-help books would make me a better person. Not necessarily stronger or fitter, but definitely wiser. And happier.

Seriously, there are many self-help books about bipolar disorder that are really useful. Here are the titles of just a few:

Bipolar 101: A practical guide to identifying triggers, managing medications, coping with symptoms and more by Ruth C. White and John D. Preston.
Bipolar disorder: A guide for patients and families by Francis Mark Mondimore.
I am not sick I don't need help! by Xavier Amador with Anna-Lisa Johanson.
Loving someone with bipolar disorder by Julie A Fast.
Mastering bipolar disorder Edited by Kerrie Eyers & Gordon Parker.
The bipolar disorder survival guide by David J. Miklowitz
The bipolar workbook: Tools for controlling your mood swings by Monica Ramirez Basco.
The depression workbook: A guide for living with depression and manic depression by Mary Ellen Copeland.
What Goes Up... Surviving the Manic Episode of a Loved One by Judy Eron.

Resilience

Sometimes people ask me what makes me resilient, and why I fight so hard to be positive in the face of challenge and adversity. This is what I tell them:

- I had a happy childhood.
- I have a great life.
- I love my husband, my children and my parents and they love me.
- When I have problems I try to be optimistic and positive.
- I look for the funny side of stressful situations.
- I have close friends I can talk to.
- I am resourceful, but I don't expect myself to be perfect.
- I am organised and flexible.
- I have skills and competencies.
- I can be courageous when I need to be.

There's a saying 'Life's not fair, get used to it.' It's true. The ones who survive, and thrive, are not those who are the smartest or strongest but the ones who can adapt to change, because adapting to change is the only real challenge in life. This is my recipe for resilience:

- Belong.
- Participate.
- Contribute.
- Collaborate and engage.
- Take any and all opportunities to affirm your strength.
- Take the initiative.
- Access all the supports that you can.
- Cultivate optimism and humour.
- Have a sense of purpose.
- Don't take everything too personally.
- Set, plan and achieve realistic goals.

- Tap into your decision making and problem solving skills.
- Be creative and flexible and accept what you cannot change, but make sure that you change what you can, even if it is only your perspective.

And if you've got bipolar disorder or depression, or any type of mental illness, when you start to feel unwell see your doctor straight away, check your medication, make sure you get enough sleep, exercise and watch what you eat, blah, blah, blah.

Try it.

(Even if I don't always do it) I am convinced it truly works.

Oranges and lemons - Oil on canvas 700 x 1000 mm

For carers

If you're a carer

I have bipolar disorder, but I am also a carer, and have been the carer of someone with a mental illness.

As a carer this is what I know…

The biggest thing you live with is fear. Fear of the illness and its consequences. Fear of the effect on your family. Fear of the unexpected. Fear of what will happen when you are no longer around.

You worry about the person you care for, and the fact that you have the life-long burden of responsibility for their care. Caring is of an all-consuming nature.

You have a sense of duty.

You are concerned and confused about what your loved one is going through.

You are really frustrated about the lack of early support.

You are worried there will never be a solution. You can get through a day, or a week, or a month, but a lifetime is going to be difficult. The problem's not going to go away, and it is going to affect all of your family members.

Sometimes you don't understand what is going on. You feel like you don't know enough about the illness, even though you have to deal with it on a daily basis.

You need support.

It can be a financial burden. Maybe you have had to give up work to be a carer. Maybe it has affected your earning capacity and you have been forced to make different choices than you otherwise would have. Maybe your employer is not understanding about your caring role. The financial burden can be a double whammy, as the person you care for may be unable to earn money either. If you live on the disability pension, it's not a lot.

Your life is not your own any more.

You may feel as though you have been 'ripped off'.

You suffer from isolation, guilt, stigma and shame. Other people have normal or perfect lives/partners/children. Nobody wants to hear about the mental illness that has hijacked your life. There are lots of people you don't/can't talk to about it. You feel excluded socially. Rather than trying to explain, it is easier/better not to say anything about it.

You feel as though you are criticised. Somehow, it is your fault that this has happened. You have been over-protective or done something wrong.

Your health suffers. You are sleep deprived, and this is a big problem. You are on alert and on guard all the time. You are constantly anxious. You are hyper-vigilant, watching … watching … watching … waiting … waiting … waiting … for the next crisis.

You don't know where to get help. You don't know where to start. You don't know what's out there. You don't know how to access it. You don't know what to do when something happens in the middle of the night.

You are isolated. Psychiatrists will (usually) only see the person you care for and you are excluded. You don't know what is going on. There are professional boundaries, and confidentially excludes you.

You fear for your other children/family members and how it is affecting them. You worry about your family breaking down (a recurring theme).

You lose your confidence.

There may be issues of abuse and violence.

You can't erase some of the the bad memories.

You grieve for so many losses – yours and theirs. Where has your life gone? Where has their life gone?

What about housing and supported accommodation?

You may have to care for the children of your own mentally ill child.

Management of medication can be difficult. What medication are they taking? Are they actually taking it? Is it the right medication? How can you help?

If your child/spouse has been in hospital, you are often given no information or support after discharge. Where is the 'after sales service'?

How do you deal with drug, alcohol and gambling problems that go hand in hand with the mental illness? These are very, very difficult issues to deal with.

You can't fix a lot of these problems.

What do you do about compulsive spending? How do you help manage someone else's finances, so that they don't get into huge financial difficulty?

You don't know how to help younger children who are living with a parent who has a mental illness.

You feel that you have no 'status' as a carer and no recognition from anyone, despite the fact you are the one living with, and dealing with the problems.

Your loved one often denies that there is anything wrong with them and they refuse to seek help.

Your child/husband makes a doctor's appointment and doesn't show up and you still have to pay for it.

You constantly 'walk on egg shells'.

You lose perspective.

You don't realise how much you need a break until you actually have one.

Carers need to be recognised as part of the solution. Our expertise should be acknowledged and valued and our input and involvement should be valued by professionals. We need to be listened to. And we need to be supported.

We need help to learn how to manage with hope rather than resignation.

If (like me) you are a carer and want some help, contact Carers Australia www.carersaustralia.com.au.

You are not on your own.

Practical tips for carers

A person with unstable bipolar disorder will rarely accept the blame for their own bad behaviour. It is always someone else's fault. They will fervently believe that the problem is not their own inappropriate behaviour, but it is your problem because you are the one who is upset and acting unreasonably (in their opinion). They will blame you for getting angry rather than accepting that their initial bad behaviour was the problem.

Some practical tips for the management of someone who has undiagnosed or uncontrolled bipolar disorder or someone who is having an 'episode' due to mental illness:

- Establish firm boundaries and structures and stick to them.
- Don't feed the problems.
- Be brief, don't reason with them.
- Communicate simply and clearly.
- Don't yell.
- Be consistent.
- Don't own their problems.

Keep calm and have a cup of tea - Charcoal on paper 200 x 300 mm

Everything carers need to know

Who cares? Lots of people care.

People care about people with mental illnesses, and people care about carers.

Carers can be parents, but they can also be children (younger children or adult children), grandparents, siblings, aunts and uncles and friends.

Carers of people with mental illness don't necessarily live with them, but they provide care and support. There are primary and secondary carers.

In this book I am talking about unpaid carers, not people who are employed in the disability sector as care workers.

I know many, many carers, and they are all remarkable people, who do a fantastic job under often difficult and challenging circumstances. However, carers should not have to, and indeed do not need to, bear the burden alone.

Some carers cope well and don't want help. Some carers want help and know how to access it. Other carers want help, but have no idea where to get it.

There is a lot of help and support available if people want it (see the back of the book).

Stages carers go through

If you suspect someone you care about has a mental illness, there will be several stages you will go through. Initially there will be a growing suspicion that things are not quite right. You will notice 'odd' behavior. It often (but not always) begins in a benign way and then escalates incrementally. However, sometimes, bizarre behaviour escalates quickly, and occasionally, a sudden onset of an episode of mental illness seems to come out of nowhere.

At first you will probably not be able to put your finger on what is wrong. You will be aware that, yes, there are problems, but they may be intermittent, or the person you care for may conceal the worst of it from you. They may not like what is happening either and feel ashamed and embarrassed at their own behaviour.

Then, after (what can be many years of) seeking support from various quarters, and seeing many different medical professionals, a diagnosis will be made. Paradoxically, this can be a relief, as you, and the person you care for, finally know what is going on and you can both start to deal with it by accessing treatment and support.

There will be a period of adjustment as you come to terms

with the diagnosis, the illness and the treatment, and work out what it means for the future. Finally there will be continuing management as you get on with your life, the best way you can.

What to do if you suspect someone you care for has a mental health problem

If you are worried that someone you care about might have a mental illness, then (in my opinion) this is what you should do:

Take them to the doctor or to a health professional. If they don't want to, insist (threaten, bribe, lie or cajole if you have to) and do it sooner rather than later.

Don't accept "I don't know" as an answer from a doctor or other health professional. If the person they see first cannot help, take them to see someone else. Persist (even if it takes years) until you get the right answer. Try one doctor after another. Persistence is the only way you will ultimately get the right help. Never give up. (Having said that, I know there are some people and situations you cannot change, no matter how hard you try, and learning to live with them is all you can do.)

After a diagnosis learn as much as you can about the illness, and what supports are available for the person, and for yourself, as quickly as possible.

Understand that the person you care for has to take responsibility for themselves and their treatment. While you can support them, you cannot not do it for them.

Don't feel guilty. What has happened is not your fault and you did not do anything to make it happen.

Realise that there is no quick fix or easy solution. It will be a long road, so pace yourself and conserve some of your energy. It may be necessary to see a psychiatrist every week for the first two or three years and every few months after that.

Set boundaries and stick to them. Do not allow yourself to become over-burdened. For example, set a limit on the number of visits or the length of time you are on the phone to them ('I can give you fifteen minutes, and then I will have to go.')

Look after yourself. If you go under, you won't be of any help to anyone else, especially the person you care for.

Strategies

If you are worried about someone you care for, and you feel that they are unwell, but you don't know what they are doing regarding treatment, or you know or suspect that they are not seeing their doctor, or they have stopped taking their medication, and they won't talk to you about it, what can you do? You may be at a complete loss about what to do, however, there are some things you can try.

One of the biggest problems for carers is lack of collaboration with medical professionals. Privacy laws mean that you cannot speak to the doctor or psychologist unless the person who has the illness agrees or requests it. If they do not, there is nothing you can do in that instance. However, there are ways to try and circumvent this problem.

Strategy #1

One strategy (which may or may not be appropriate or achievable) is to discuss your concerns with the person that you care for (when the situation is calm) and say you are worried and would like to help. You can ask them if it would be possible for you to come with them to a doctor's appointment and spend a short time with the doctor just talking about the condition, not about them personally, or their situation or private business. Assure them that you only want to discuss the diagnosis in general terms with the doctor and find out what you can do to help.

If they agree to this, and if you can, the best thing to do (again when the situation is calm, well prior to an appointment) is to get them to jot down a brief note addressed to the doctor, saying, for example, 'I give permission for Dr X to discuss bipolar disorder in general with my mother/wife/carer and also talk to her about how she can help. I do/do not give permission for Dr. X to discuss (specific aspects of) my personal situation. Signed...'

Discussing this prior to the appointment and getting written agreement and consent before you go to the appointment means that the doctor can be clear about what information he/she can legally disclose. The boundaries are clearly established before your visit and it empowers both you and the person you care for. Because the note can be given to the doctor's secretary with the referral, the doctor is able to read it before you go in to see him/her. This prevents any awkwardness for you, for the person who is with you and for the doctor. The person you care for will sometimes actually disclose additional helpful information to you during or after the appointment.

I know of quite a few situations where this strategy has been extremely successful.

Strategy #2

A second strategy is to ask if you can take the person to the doctor, with the aim (as you will explain) of eliminating suspicion that there is a serious problem. In other words, you tell the person you care for that you are not going because there is a problem; you are going because you want to confirm that there isn't one.

Strategy #3

A third strategy is to offer to drive the person to the appointment, and then regardless of whether you can talk to the doctor or not, plan (in advance) a really nice outing afterwards, such as lunch, a shopping expedition, a trip to the art gallery/beach/ movies or so on.

If there is a relaxed, enjoyable shared (non-threatening and non-adversarial) activity after the appointment, sometimes people will open up naturally and talk about their situation. If not, you have not lost anything, and gained a nice day out.

When nothing works

Often the person you care for will not agree to even discuss any of the above. They will not give permission for you to talk to the doctor or have anything to do with their medical appointments. Sometimes you know the name of the diagnosis and/or the medication they have been prescribed. Sometimes you don't even know that.

Many times the person is in denial and will not entertain the idea of seeing anyone at all, or the suggestion that anything is wrong.

In this case, the only thing you can do is persevere. Gently, but persistently, try to encourage them to seek treatment. Talk to your own GP about the situation.

If things get out of hand and you are really worried, do not hesitate to call the area mental health team or the hospital. It is better to be safe (and embarrassed), than sorry (and have regrets).

One of the biggest problems is where to find a good psychiatrist in the first place. Of course, your GP should be able to refer you to someone, and if it is urgent, they may even call a specialist on your behalf and try to get you an early appointment.

Word of mouth is a really good way of finding out about who might be a good psychiatrist for your loved one. There are support groups for people with bipolar disorder and other mental illnesses where families and friends are welcome and encouraged to come with their loved one or on their own.

Support groups are not in the business of making referrals or recommendations, but the people who attend have a wealth of information. Informally, over a cup of tea and a biscuit, they share all sorts of things with each other.

When you finally see a psychiatrist, if you don't 'click' with them, go back to your GP and ask to be referred to someone else. I cannot stress enough how important it is to have confidence in the psychiatrist you are seeing. Many people go through a number of specialists before finding the right 'fit'.

Also, some psychiatrists specialise in specific areas of mental health, for example bipolar disorder and ADHD, or bipolar disorder and addictions, or mental health and adolescents. They have a special interest and expertise in these areas.

Whatever the situation you find yourself in as a carer, you can obtain information about mental illness in general and specific illnesses such as bipolar disorder from a variety of sources. You can also access practical and emotional support for yourself. See the back of the book for information about support organisations.

What carers want and need

Carers want and need the following:

- to be able to work collaboratively with the health professionals treating those they care about
- to be included in the process

- to have their expertise, experience and input acknowledged and valued
- to be able to access information and support from professionals and from mental health organisations
- to have their own personal support networks (for example, personal friends and family members, or people they meet at support groups)
- to have breaks from their caring roll
- to be able to talk about being a carer
- to have understanding and appreciation from the community
- to have hope for the future.

Most of all, carers want, and need, to know (and to be told) that they are doing the best they can, in fact, that they are doing a fantastic job (because they are). Carers are critical for those with mental illnesses but also for society in general.

'In 2010 Carers Australia commissioned Access Economics to undertake an Australian study of the economic value of the informal care provided by unpaid family carers for people with disability, mental illness, chronic conditions, terminal illness and the frail aged. That report found that the value of informal care exceeded $40 billion per annum in 2010. This was based on the replacement cost of care of $31 per hour.

A huge proportion of this cost was due to demographic ageing, but mental illness significantly contributed to the increasing number of Australians who required and received care.

Informal carers (overall) now provide over 1.32 billion hours of care each year, and represent a precious economic resource.'

(*The economic value of informal care in 2010*, Access Economics report for Carers Australia).

As a community we need to appreciate our carers. A little validation goes a long way.

A little validation - Charcoal on paper 200 x 300 mm

Where carers can get support

There are many amazing organisations that provide comprehensive information and useful support specifically for carers. Carers can contact them at any stage, from their early niggling concerns, through to a formal diagnosis and on to managing a chronic and difficult illness.

Some of these organisations are listed at the back of this book. Many of them have large databases of information about other organizations

In addition to formal support there are informal groups where carers can meet and talk about (or not talk about) their situation with others who are going through the same things and who fully understand and empathise. These can also be found in the within the databases of the organisations listed.

Something for carers to think about

A person living with (or going through an episode of) a severe mental illness cannot easily conceptualise, let alone articulate their thoughts and feelings. If they could talk about it with you, this is what they might say:

> 'I have not chosen to be like this and if I could be well I would be. I don't drink to excess and or take drugs to spite you and I don't stop taking my medication or avoid treatment just to be willful and difficult. When I am ill I simply don't have any insight.'

They would tell you how difficult it is to relinquish their fundamental belief in their identity as a 'normal' person.

How to help someone who has a mental illness

What is helpful?

Recognise that:

- Recovery will take time.
- Rest is important.
- Things will get better.
- Space is important.
- It's OK to offer, it's OK to refuse.
- It will help to try and ignore what you can't change.
- It is a good idea to temporarily lower your expectations and use personal yardsticks, for example, comparing this week/month to last week/month.
- People with depression are not lazy or weak, and it is not true that if they tried hard enough they could 'snap out of it'.
- Having depression is extremely isolating and often people withdraw from social contact.
- Mental illness is not something to be fearful of.
- Even if someone 'looks OK', they may feel unwell, so be sensitive and empathetic.

What is unhelpful?

- Judging disclosures negatively and/or being punitive.
- Viewing difficulties as 'attention seeking'.
- Making assumptions about behavior.

- Treating the person as though they have an intellectual impairment.
- Being in denial and ignoring the problem or hitting the 'panic button' prematurely.
- Using the person's diagnosis or illness to exert power or control over them, for example in an argument, or joking about the person having a 'bipolar moment'.
- Diminishing the disorder.

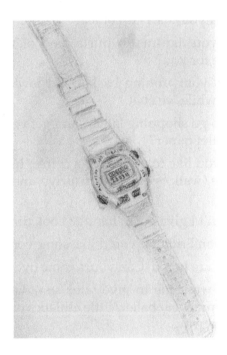

Time - Pencil on paper 100 x 200 mm

What can you say?

When I was depressed, nothing anyone said or did could really help, but sometimes people did make me feel better and my life a little easier. They said things like:

- It's good to see you.
- I am sorry to hear you are (or your loved one is) not well.

- This depression/bipolar disorder/mental illness must be difficult.
- Do you want to talk about it?
- You know I support you one hundred percent.
- I will do whatever it takes to help you through this.
- This isn't your fault.
- Here's a casserole for your dinner tonight.
- I've brought you some magazines.
- Can I get you/us a cup of tea?
- Would you like me to put a load of washing in the machine for you?
- Where's your ironing basket? I'd love to do a bit of ironing while we chat.
- I have to go shopping later. Can I get you some bread/milk/toilet paper?
- Would you like to go out for a coffee/lunch/massage/pedicure/walk/swim? I can drive and it will be my shout.
- Why don't I give you a hand to cook dinner?
- I'm free on Friday if you'd like some company.
- My kids are bored. Can yours come over to play?
- Do you want me to give your son/daughter a lift to football practice/ballet/little athletics on Saturday? I'm going anyway.

What not to say

When I was depressed, I found it difficult to interact with others. I did not want to go out and I hated talking on the phone. Yet I felt I had to make an effort to 'look' and 'be' normal. So when I did have to go to the supermarket and the girl on the checkout asked me how I was, I would say 'fine' even though I wasn't. When I bumped into people I knew, I didn't know what to say.

They would say light-hearted or positive things. I am sure they were trying to make me feel better and their intentions were good but their comments often showed a complete lack of understanding of what I was going through. It is difficult, because if you haven't experienced depression yourself, how can you know what to say or not to say? At the time I felt they were being insensitive and demeaning, although I am sure this was not their intent.

I think it was more about my sensitivity and the negative space I was trapped in rather than the things people were saying. It is only with hindsight that I understand. It is only with hindsight that I can see that people were genuinely trying to be helpful and empathetic.

The $64,000 question: Is it better to say nothing and pretend everything is fine?
The simple answer: No.

In my opinion it is much better for you to say something rather than ignore it, even if it is the 'wrong' thing. You want to be kind, helpful and sympathetic, you just don't know what to say or do and you feel uncomfortable and awkward. If what you say comes from good intentions and a kind heart, it might be stupid, but how can it be wrong?

There are a few things I can tell you though. It is very important for you to understand that you cannot 'jolly' someone out of a state of clinical depression. You cannot fix it so don't attempt to 'problem solve'. You cannot judge the other person by how you are feeling, or by how you think you would feel in their situation.

Don't trivialise what they are going through by offering platitudes such as:

- You'll be right (maybe they won't).
- Just think happy thoughts (it isn't that simple).
- I know just how you feel (no you don't).
- I've been a bit depressed myself lately (not like this).
- Stop feeling sorry for yourself (you would in the same situation).
- You are very self-absorbed at the moment (it goes with the territory).

- You've got it better than most, (yes, but knowing that doesn't help).
- Get a grip/get over it/cheer up/look on the bright side (they're trying to).
- Stop obsessing about your problems, just don't think about them (it's impossible).
- You should see my…naturopath, chiropractor, therapist, etc. (they might help, but there is no easy fix for this).
- You should take…herbal remedies, St John's Wort, vitamin C D E … (they won't cure this).
- Just try a bit harder (they can't).
- You need to get out more (they don't want to).
- Are you sure you're depressed, you don't look depressed to me? (are you a doctor?).
- I'm surprised at you, I thought you were stronger than that (they are, the illness is just stronger).
- What have you got to be depressed about? (nothing, that's the problem).
- Why don't you try the gym? (they will, when they feel better).
- If you don't like feeling like this, then just make up your mind and change the way you are feeling (it is not a matter of will).
- Lighten up, it's not that bad (actually, it is).
- If you hadn't gone to see that psychiatrists you'd be fine (no they wouldn't).
- Life wasn't meant to be easy (no, it wasn't, for any of us).

What else not to say:

Nothing.
Don't say nothing.

Say something, even if you feel awkward or embarrassed. The person will then give you a clue as to where to take the conversation from there. And if your words are not well

172

received then, maybe they will be appreciated later. And if not later, at least you tried.

Nothing comes from nothing.

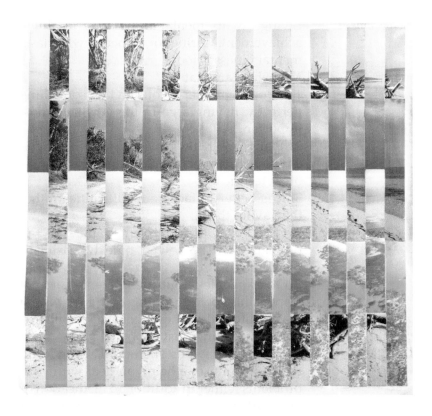

Happy thoughts - Photographic collage 380 x 410 mm

My A to Z of mental illness

Achievement: Living with mental illness is a huge achievement. Caring for someone who has a mental illness is too.

Beliefs: My beliefs are that:

1. It doesn't matter if you can't do something perfectly, having a go in life is what's most important.

2. Plans don't always work out how you envisage them, but what does happen is often terrific too.

3. It is better to face your difficulties rather than avoid them.

4. Everyone has problems and not all problems can be solved quickly, easily or painlessly.

5. Other people or outside influences are not responsible for everything that goes wrong in your life and neither is your mental illness. Sometimes things just happen.

CBT: Cognitive Behaviour Therapy is a wonderful tool you can use to help you deal with your problems (either in addition to medication or by itself). You can learn how to change your thinking, behaviour and emotional responses to gain a better perspective on many issues.

Drugs: If bipolar disorder is in your family you may be predisposed to getting it yourself. Be aware that taking illicit drugs (especially marijuana) can trigger bipolar disorder, and once that has happened, it is too late to go back and undo it. Why take the risk?

Encouragement: Seek out support and cherish it when and where you find it.

Friends: People with bipolar disorder need all the friends they can get.

Gunna's & Doers:	Be a 'doer', not a 'gunna'. Whatever your goals are, take action now.
Happiness:	You don't have to be happy to be positive, resilient and strong.
Imagination:	Visualise.
Inertia:	Get up. Show up. Start.
Jokes:	Find things to laugh about.
Knowledge:	Knowledge is power.
Love:	Love is everything.
Motivation:	Motivation can only come from within.
Mindfulness:	Practise mindfulness and meditation. Live in the moment, pay attention and be aware. Spend time in contemplation and reflection.
Nice:	How to be nice:
	Give other people your undivided attention. Put yourself in other people's shoes and consider the situation from their point of view.
	Give other people the benefit of the doubt and don't automatically think the worst of them.
	Don't let your moods impact on other people. Try to recognize when you are in a bad mood and work to keep that mood from affecting how you treat others (this is not easy when you have bipolar disorder).
	Act on nice thoughts and ideas. When you feel the urge to say something nice or to do something for someone, do it. Often times when you do not act on the opportunity to be nice to others, you will not get another chance.
Opportunity:	Create your own opportunities.
Persistence:	Don't give up. Never stop trying to: get help; find the right doctor; work out the best treatment; and live well with bipolar disorder. It can be done.
Problems:	In my observation, people are worrying about big problems, like having cancer or being unemployed or getting a divorce. If they don't have any big problems to worry about,

they worry about middle size problems, like their house renovations or having a baby or a shitty job. If they don't have any middle sized problems to worry about, they worry about little problems like what their kids are up to, or where they are going for Christmas or why they can't afford a new lounge. And if they don't have any little problems they invent some. From what I can see, a lot of people expend the same amount of energy worrying about the big problems as the non-existent ones.

Quantum leap: It is a quantum leap from denial to acceptance, to acknowledgement that, *yes*, you do have a mental illness and *yes*, you do have to deal with it.

Responsibility: Be accountable for your own actions. You might have bipolar disorder, but you still have choices. Don't make excuses.

Success: You have been given special talents. Don't squander them.

Truth: Every person has their own version of the truth.

Understand: Understand that you can reinvent yourself, if you really want to.

Vision: There's always 20/20 vision with hindsight.

Warning signs: You might think something is not quite right, or someone else might tell you that they are concerned about you. Even if you think there's nothing wrong, listen to them. Humour them. Go to the doctor and get yourself checked out. What harm can it do?

Wisdom: Learn from your mistakes and don't beat yourself up over them.

X Factor: Some (intelligent, creative, unique) people with bipolar disorder have it. You can too.

Yell: Sometimes it helps to yell.

Zest for life: What this book is all about.

Zest for life - Oil on canvas 500 x 600 mm

Where to get help

My website and blog

I have a website at www.atnaylor.com and a blog at becauseofbipolar.com.au. Some of my blog posts are about bipolar disorder, but some are not. Everything in my life is coloured by bipolar disorder, so even when I blog about things that seem totally unrelated, they are connected in some way.

I hope that all readers of my blog get something out of it, whether they have a mental illness or not.

I set up a blog because when I mention that I have bipolar disorder, people often (furtively) approach me, wanting to talk about it. And not just bipolar disorder. They want to talk about depression, anxiety, OCD, ADHD, eating disorders and so on.

Mental illness is really out there (even though it is not 'out' there, if you know what I mean).

People want to know more about bipolar disorder than I can tell them in a brief, private conversation. They have partners or children with mental health issues. They tell me they are desperate to find out more about it. They have so many questions and the more I tell them, the more they want to know.

I can (and do) refer them to books, organisations and resources, but they want to hear personal stories.

They want to hear my stories.

As I write posts for this blog, I sometimes wonder why I write them. One of my friends said, '*Who would want to read about you?*' She's right, of course. It's very self-indulgent. So why do I write my blog?

I write to please myself. I write because I like writing. I write because I get a great deal of satisfaction from being able to publish my work every day (albeit on a blog site).

I write because I like talking about bipolar disorder, and there are not many places in my life I can discuss mental illness. I also write my blog to connect with people — my friends, other writers and artists, people who also have bipolar disorder and carers. Anyone really.

Because I have bipolar disorder I am part of a minority community. I am also a carer (another minority community) and a writer (yet another). As with any minority group, there are experiences I have in common with other people in that group. I have a sense of belonging and kinship that I do not have outside that community. I also feel this sense of kinship when I read the blogs of others who also have bipolar disorder.

Bipolar disorder aside, I started the blog because I love to write.

Words have power. My words do and yours do too.

Information, support and advocacy agencies and websites

This is not a complete or comprehensive directory, rather a list of personal favourites. The organisations, agencies and websites listed here have many contacts and links that you might find helpful. Every effort has been made to ensure that the information is accurate, however details may have changed since publication.

Anxiety Online
www.anxietyonline.org.au

Anxiety Online is a comprehensive online mental health service offering information, assessment, online diagnosis and treatment programs ("eTherapy") for the following anxiety disorders: Generalised Anxiety Disorder; Social Anxiety Disorder; Obsessive Compulsive Disorder; Post-Traumatic Stress Disorder and Panic Disorder with or without Agoraphobia.

beyondblue
1300 22 4636 (info line for depression and anxiety and where to get help)
www.beyondblue.org.au
www.youthbeyondblue.org.au (Youth *beyondblue*)

beyondblue, the national depression and anxiety initiative, aims to raise awareness and understanding, and provide clear and comprehensive information about, depression, anxiety and related disorders, available treatments and where to get help.

BlueVoices is *beyondblue*'s consumer and carer reference group. Consultation with blueVoices members is an integral part of *beyondblue*'s success in raising awareness across Australia and reducing the stigma associated with depression and anxiety. Anyone in Australia with personal experiences of depression, anxiety, pre- and postnatal depression/anxiety or bipolar disorder can join blueVoices. The group also includes carers, family members and friends who care for and support people with these illnesses.

BIPOLAR Education Foundation
02 8116 3289
www.bipolar-edu.org

The BIPOLAR Education Foundation delivers tailored mental health presentations to the community. This includes high schools, community organisations, businesses and sporting clubs, aiming at creating more accepting schoolyards, positive and understanding workplaces encouraging self-responsibility and making informed choices. BEF is about Education, Awareness and Destigmatisation of mental illness promoting "an early diagnosis".

BluePages Depression Information
www.bluepages.anu.edu.au

This website was developed and delivered by the Australian National University and contains comprehensive, evidence-based information about depression and its treatment (including medical, psychological and alternative therapies). BluePages Depression Information also includes interactive depression and anxiety quizzes, descriptions of the experience and symptoms of depression, a relaxation download, and extensive resources for help.

Black Dog Institute
02 9382 4530
www.blackdoginstitute.org.au

The Black Dog Institute offers specialist mood disorders assessment, treatment and information. It contributes to research in the area and offers education programs. There is also a list of Australian support groups for consumers and carers on its website.

bphope
www.bphope.com

The (American) bphope magazine offers bipolar disorder information, support and resources about bipolar disorder for patients, family and friends. They publish four issues annually.

CADE Clinic
02 9926 7746
www.cadeclinic.com

The CADE Clinic provides specialist clinical assessment and diagnostic evaluation of common mental health problems. The clinic, affiliated with the Discipline of Psychiatry, University of Sydney, is an outpatient service that is based at the Department of Academic Psychiatry at Royal North Shore Hospital. It offers a detailed clinical appraisal of depression, bipolar disorder, anxiety disorders, and other psychiatric and psychological disorders. In addition to a clinical service, they conduct a wide range of research using neuroimaging and neuropsychological tests and assess treatments for mood and anxiety disorders, and other psychiatric disorders including schizophrenia.

Carers Australia
02 6122 9900
1800 242 636
www.carersaustralia.com.au

Carers Australia is the national peak body representing Australia's 2.6 million unpaid carers. Carers Australia advocates on behalf of Australia's unpaid carers to influence policies, programs and services at a national level. They also manage a range of national programs that support unpaid carers in their caring role. All carers in Australia can contact the Carer Line on 1800 242 636 for emotional support, advice, information and referrals. This service is delivered by the carer association in each state and territory.

Carers NSW and Young Carers NSW
1800 242 636
www.carersnsw.asn.au
www.youngcarersnsw.asn.au

Carers NSW is an association for relatives and friends caring for people with a disability, mental illness, drug and alcohol dependencies, chronic conditions, terminal illness or who are frail. They are the peak organisation for carers in New South Wales, Australia.

Crazy Meds
www.crazymeds.us

Crazy Meds is a website where you can learn what's good, what's bad, what's interesting, and what's plain weird and funny about the medications used to treat depression, bipolar disorder, schizophrenia, epilepsy, migraines, anxiety, neuropathic pain, or whatever psychiatric and/or neurological condition you might have. The information on this site is to help you work with your doctor(s) to find the right treatment options.

dNet – People Like Us (formerly depressioNet)
depressioNet.org.au

The purpose of dNet is to empower 'people like us' to make informed choices and find solutions to the challenges of living with depression. Here you will find a comprehensive resource for information, help to access professionals, treatments, tools, etc., throughout Australia, and peer support in the message board and chat rooms.

FyrenIyce
www.fyreniyce.org

The bipolar website FyrenIyce offers information about diagnosis, symptoms, treatment and treatment concerns, research, resources and addresses the real life issues and concerns of people dealing with bipolar disorder. There is also an email and real time support list.

headspace
03 9027 0100
www.headspace.org.au

Headspace offers support, information and health services for young people (age 12-25) with mental health problems and their families at 30 centres throughout Australia.

Lifeline
13 11 14
www.lifeline.org.au

Lifeline provides access to 24 hour telephone crisis support on 13 11 14 or chat one-on-one with a Lifeline Online Crisis Supporter (8pm – midnight, 7 days a week). For more information or to download mental health and suicide prevention resources visit www.lifeline.org.au

Living Is For Everyone (LIFE)
03 8398 8422
www.livingisforeveryone.com.au

Living Is For Everyone (LIFE) is an initiative funded by the Department of Health and Ageing under the National Suicide Prevention Strategy (NSPS). It provides information and resources on suicide and suicide prevention for professionals, including the LIFE Framework which guides national and local suicide prevention activities.

Mental Health Association NSW
02 9339 6000
1300 794 991 Mental Health Information Service
1300 794 992 Anxiety Disorders Information Service
www.mentalhealth.asn.au

The Mental Health Association of NSW plays a vital role in the development of mental health initiatives, which result in increased community awareness and knowledge of mental health issues. With the support of their Board, staff, members, volunteers and students, they work towards a society free from prejudice and discrimination against people living with mental illness. The Mental Health Association of NSW strives towards a community that embraces and maintains mental, social and emotional wellbeing for all people.

Mental Illness Fellowship of Australia (MIFA)
1800 985 944
www.mifa.org.au

MIFA is a non-government, not-for-profit organisation aimed at supporting and advocating for people with serious mental illnesses and their families. It has member organisations in most Australian states that offer education and services to enhance the quality of life of people affected by mental illness and those who care for them. Apart from numerous information resources, they offer supportive, rehabilitation and recovery based programs.

Mental Health in Multicultural Australia (MHiMA)
1300 136 289
www.mhima.org.au

MHiMA is funded by the Australian Government to promote mental health and prevent suicide amongst culturally and linguistically diverse groups (CALD) in Australia. It provides information for carers and consumers about mental health issues, the mental health system, personal stories and articles and resources. Information and factsheets about mental illness and ways to deal with it are available in various languages. There are also reference groups and self-help groups for carers and the same for consumers. Consumer Advisory Groups enable consumers to help plan mental health services and policy.

SANE Australia
Helpline 1800 18 SANE (7263)
www.sane.org

SANE offers helpful information and support for people with bipolar disorder, family and friends. They also focus on improving the overall health of people with mental illness. SANE campaigns for better services and attitudes towards people with mental illness. They answer questions that people have about mental illness via their 1800 and online helpline.

There is also support with preventing suicide and guidelines for those working with people who have lost a loved one.

Schizophrenia Fellowship of NSW
1800 985 944
www.sfnsw.org.au

The Schizophrenia Fellowship of NSW is committed to improving the circumstances and welfare of people with a serious mental illness, their relatives and carers and providing support for professionals working in the area. The Schizophrenia Fellowship works to eliminate stigma, to ensure that people have access to information and appropriate services, to advocate on behalf of people with a serious mental illness (in particular schizophrenia) and to lobby for better government policy in the areas of research, treatment, rehabilitation and housing.

Siblings Australia
www.siblingsaustralia.org.au

This national organisation aims to enhance the wellbeing of siblings of adults and children with a mental illness, disability or chronic physical illness. They provide information, workshops and networking opportunities.

South Pacific Private
1800 063 332
www.southpacificprivate.com.au

South Pacific Private is a treatment centre in Curl Curl, Sydney, NSW, Australia that provides support for people who have problems with addiction and mood disorders. They provide support and education and offer inpatient, day and evening treatment programs.

Suicide Call Back Service
1300 659 467
www.suicidecallbackservice.org.au

The Suicide Call Back Service is a free nationwide telephone support service, staffed by real people with professional qualifications. Operated 24/7, this service is available to people at risk of suicide, carers for someone who is suicidal and anyone bereaved by suicide.

Suicide Prevention Australia
02 9223 3333
www.suicidepreventionaust.org

Suicide Prevention Australia is the national peak body for the suicide prevention sector in Australia. They promote collaboration, coordination and partnerships in suicide prevention, intervention and postvention. Their mission is to make suicide prevention everybody's business.

Transcultural Mental Health Centre
1800 648 911
www.dhi.health.nsw.gov.au/tmhc

'The Transcultural Mental Health Centre (TMHC) is a NSW statewide service that promotes access to mental health services for people of culturally and linguistically diverse (CALD) backgrounds. TMHC is a leader in cross cultural clinical consultation and assessment, transcultural mental health promotion, prevention and early intervention, publication and resource development and education and training.

The Wayside Chapel
02 9581 9100
www.thewaysidechapel.com

The Wayside Chapel provides unconditional love and support for people on and around the streets of Kings Cross in Sydney, NSW and has done so since 1964. Many of these people have endured lives of great hardship and struggle with alcohol and other drug addictions, mental illness and homelessness.

With wings you can fly

Famous people who have bipolar disorder

Famous and creative people who have bipolar disorder (according to online encyclopedia Wikipedia) include:

- Sophie Anderton, model
- Adam Ant, musician
- Emilie Autumn, musician
- Andy Behrman, author
- Max Bemis, musician Say Anything
- Maurice Benard, actor
- Ludwig Boltzmann, mathematician
- Adrian Borland, British musician
- Russell Brand, actor
- Andrea Breth, stage director
- Jeremy Brett, actor
- Frank Bruno, boxer
- Robert Calvert, musician
- Alastair Campbell, press advisor
- Georg Cantor, mathematician
- Dick Cavett, television journalist
- Iris Chang, historian
- John Clare, poet
- Kurt Cobain, musician Nirvana
- Neil Cole, politician
- Rosemary Clooney, singer and actress
- Patricia Cornwell, writer
- Robert S. Corrington, theologist

- Michael Costa, politician
- Vincent Crane, keyboardist
- Ray Davies, musician
- Mike Doughty, musician
- Charmaine Dragun, Australian journalist
- Richard Dreyfuss, legendary actor
- Patty Duke, actress
- Disco D, record producer
- Carrie Fisher, Star Wars actress and writer
- Connie Francis, singer
- Stephen Fry, actor, writer, comedian
- Justin Furstenfeld, lead singer Blue October
- Alan Garner, novelist
- Paul Gascoigne, English footballer
- Mel Gibson, actor and director
- Mathew Good, Canadian musician
- Philip Graham, publisher
- Macy Gray, musician
- Graham Greene, English novelist
- Ivor Gurney, English composer
- Terry Hall, lead singer The Specials
- Linda Hamilton, Terminator actress
- Mariette Hartley, actress
- Jonathan Hay, Australian footballer
- Ernest Hemingway, writer
- Kristin Hersh, musician
- Abbie Hoffman, political activist
- Marya Hornbacher, writer
- Jack Irons, drummer formerly of Red Hot Chili Peppers
- Kay Redfield Jamison psychologist, activist, author
- Daniel Johnston, musician

- Andrew Johns, Rugby player
- Lee Joon, Korean actor and musician
- Chris Kanyon, American wrestler
- Kerry Katona, English tv star
- Rep. Patrick Kennedy, politician, member of Kennedy family
- Otto Klemperer, conductor
- Margot Kidder, Superman actress
- Patrick Kroupa, writer and hacker
- Vivien Leigh, Gone With The Wind actress
- Jennifer Lewis, actress
- Bill Lichtenstein, print and broadcast journalist
- Jack London, American author
- Demi Lovato, actress, singer, Disney star
- Arthur McIntyre, Australian artist
- Kristy McNichol, actress
- Burgess Meredith, actor from Batman television show
- Eric Millegan, actor
- Kate Millett, author
- Spike Milligan, comedian
- Ben Moody, musician
- Seaneen Molloy, Northern Irish blogger
- John A. Mulheren, American investor and financier
- Edvard Munch, artist
- Robert Munsch, author
- Florence Nightingale, nurse and legendary health campaigner
- Sinead O'Connor, musician
- Graeme Obree, Scottish racing cyclist
- Phil Ochs, musician
- Bill Oddie, naturalist, comic, television presenter

- Ozzy Osbourne, singer
- Cheri Oteri, Saturday Night Live actress
- Craig Owens, singer for Chiodos
- Nicola Pagett, actor
- Emma Parker Bowles, model
- Jaco Pastorius, jazz musician
- Jane Pauley, television host, journalist
- Edgar Allen Poe, legendary poet
- Jackson Pollock, American artist
- Odean Pope, jazz musician
- Gail Porter, British TV presenter
- Emil Post, mathematician
- Charley Pride, country music artist
- Rene Rivkin, entrepreneur
- Barret Robbins, NFL Pro Bowler
- Axl Rose, lead singer Guns N Roses
- Richard Rossi, filmmaker, musician, minister
- Robert Schumann, German composer
- Nina Simone, American singer
- Michael Slater, Australian cricketer
- Tony Slattery, actor and comedian
- Sidney Sheldon, producer, writer
- Tim Smith, rugby player
- Peter Steele, lead singer Type O Negative
- David Strickland, actor
- Poly Styrene, singer
- Stuart Sutherland, British psychologist and writer
- Mackenzie Taylor, British comedian
- Michael Thalbourne, Australian psychologist
- Steven Thomas, entrepreneur
- Gene Tierney, legendary actress

- Devin Townsend, musician
- Nick Traina, singer, son of Danielle Steel
- Timothy Treadwell, environmentalist
- Margaret Trudeau, Canadian celebrity
- Jean Claude Van Damme, action star actor
- Vincent Van Gogh, legendary artist
- Townes Van Zandt, singer and songwriter
- Mark Vonnegut, author
- Ruby Wax, comedian
- Scott Weiland, musician from Stone Temple Pilots
- Pete Wentz, musician Fall Out Boy
- Delonte West, business executive from The Informant
- Brian Wilson, musician The Beach Boys
- Amy Winehouse, late legendary singer
- Virginia Woolf, legendary writer
- Catherine Zeta Jones, actress

Other Prose @ IP

Frenchmans Cap: Story of a Mountain, *by Simon Kleinig*
ISBN 9781922120052, AU$33

The Terrorist, *by Barry Levy*
ISBN 9781922120076, AU$33

Blood, *by Peter Kay*
ISBN 9781922120038, AU$30

The Girl with the Cardboard Port, *by Judith L. McNeil*
ISBN 9781922120090, AU$33

No One's Child, *by Judith L. McNeil*
ISBN 9781922120151, AU$33

Write My Face, *by Kathy Sutcliffe*
ISBN 9781922120014, AU$33

Shadow Patterns, *by Daphne Tuttle*
ISBN 9781921869846, AU$33

The Rag Boiler's Daughter, *by Lois Shepheard*
ISBN 9781921869389, AU$30

Yellowcake Springs, *by Guy Salvidge*
ISBN 9781921869174, AU$33

Schadenvale Road, *by Chris Mansell*
ISBN 9781921479946, AU$30

Saved by the Bomb, *by Eric Leadbetter*
ISBN 9781921869198, AU$26.95

For the latest from IP, please visit us online at
http://ipoz.biz/Store/Store.htm
*or contact us by **phone/fax** on 61 7 3324 9319*
or sales@ipoz.biz